A
Path to
Providence

A Path to Providence

Benjamin G. Wallace, PM
P. Shaun Bradshaw, PGM

Grand Lodge of North Carolina, AF & AM

First edition published 2021

Cover design by *Ryan J. Flynn*
Title page design by *Ryan J. Flynn*
Reality vs. Probability Matrix design by *Brantleigh T. Bradshaw*
Portrait of Shaun Bradshaw by *Genesis Photography Group*
Portraits of Randy Browning, III and Ben Wallace by *Kevin Combs*
Portrait of Mike Daniels by *Allen Allred*
Portrait of Matthew Parker by *Matthew Parker*
Publishing Editor: *Jason E. Marshall*

ISBN: 978-1-7326214-2-8 (paperback)

Published by
The Laudable Pursuit Press
Norman, Oklahoma
www.TheLaudablePursuit.com
Editor@TheLaudablePursuit.com

www.TheLaudablePursuit.com

Dedication

From Bro. Ben -

Darla Bruton Wallace is the reason I can sit here writing this dedication page. She has sacrificed for Freemasonry. The countless nights and weekends she handled the kids, dinner, dogs, cats, chickens, power outages, business decisions, and major and minor emergencies of all sorts while I was off "playing Mason" as she calls it, is a testament to her resolve and that of thousands of other Masonic wives. She has been my counselor, motivator, and inspiration. She is my biggest fan and my harshest critic. She can crush my ego or my ideas and then "stoop and build them up with worn out tools." Like many wives, she has a love-hate relationship with the fraternity. But in the end, Freemasonry found a roundabout way to make our connection greater than it has ever been. For that, the Craft has my appreciation, but I promise…all of the credit goes to Darla. I love you and wholeheartedly dedicate my contributions to this to book you.

From Bro. Shaun -

Throughout my tenure as Grand Master, I shared my story – how I was raised by my mother and grandmother with no real father figure in the home. Although neither my mother nor grandmother are alive today, their departure from this earthly plane has not diminished their presence with me. I have no doubt of their continued influence and guidance as I travel along this life's path. They both knew my love for the fraternity and understood my attraction to the esoteric and philosophical aspects of Freemasonry. While they would not have used the exact same words, they absolutely raised me to believe in, and act on, Brotherly Love, Relief and Truth. I love and miss them both and dedicate this book to each of them for the many sacrifices they made to provide the best possible upbringing they could for me.

Acknowledgements

They say, "nothing worthwhile is easy" and writing this book was more difficult and time consuming than we imagined when we started down this path that Providence laid out for us. But of course, this was a worthwhile endeavor and not one either of us could have completed without the mentorship, assistance, support, and love from so many of our brethren, friends, and family.

We would like to thank Walter Leslie Wilmshurt, George H. Steinmetz, Dr. James T. Tresner, II, and W. Kirk MacNulty who, through their writings, lectures, and presentations preserved Freemasonry's original essence and style. We would also like to thank Robert G. Davis, Chuck R. Dunning, Jr., and Robert Herd who proved the essence of our Craft still lives, and can be found, if you know where to search.

To the Middle Chamber staff members, new and old: J. Randolph "Randy" Browning, III, Michael T. Daniels, Marcus S. Orr, Matthew N. Parker, J. Currie Pendleton, Anthony J. Rathbone, Michael A. Register, and Kenneth W. Wical. You are our friends, brothers, and mentors. You are whisky loving, cigar smoking, Masonic philosophers and we love you. Freemasonry would be less, and this book could not exist, without you.

To the leadership of the Grand Lodge of North Carolina, which has consistently proven itself to be progressive and proactive. Our leaders consistently demonstrate the difference between leading and managing and know, as a leader, you cannot always "play it safe." In the words of Most Worshipful D. MacLauchlin "Mack" Sigmon, the Grand Lodge of North Carolina "strives to make Masons, not members." We especially want to acknowledge Most Worshipful Douglas L. Caudle who encouraged and participated in the development of the early esoteric workshop, which evolved into the Middle Chamber Program.

Last, but certainly not least, we wish to thank all of our teachers, entities, and mentors who played a role in our personal and spiritual development. Their influence played a key role in the formation of the Middle Chamber Program. We never know what small part our life's contribution will play in the larger schemes of Providence or what will follow in the future.

Along with the individuals recognized above, Ben and Shaun would like to add the following acknowledgements and thanks.

From Bro. Ben -

I was raised to the Sublime Degree of Master Mason at Blackmer Lodge No. 127 in Mt. Gilead, North Carolina. It is a typical small town, rural lodge. It is composed of a fine group of brethren who did a respectable job of raising me, for which I will be eternally grateful. Throughout my degrees and coaching my intuition told me there was a different style of Freemasonry out there, one which I yearned to find. It took a while, but eventually a path began to emerge.

Larry Thompson and Bill Bruton pushed me to new Masonic experiences within North Carolina. Andrew Hammer inspired me with his book Observing the Craft. Enlightenment Lodge No. 198 in Colorado and the crew there demonstrated how Masonry could be spiritualized. Guthrie Scottish Rite taught me the grandeur of our degree work. Ezekiel Bates Lodge in Attleboro, MA taught me fraternity. Slowly it all began to come together.

Lastly, I want to thank our Middle Chamber patron and my co-author, Most Worshipful P. Shaun Bradshaw. You exemplify everything a Freemason should aspire to be.

Caritas,
Ben

From Bro. Shaun -

My journey as a Freemason began on a fateful Saturday at Suzie's Diner in Kernersville, NC. My college roommate, Chris Wright, his father, Ted, and I grabbed a quick bite to eat there when I noticed Ted's Masonic ring. I immediately asked him about the fraternity and knew Providence was hard at work on me when I saw his eyes light up as he talked about Freemasonry. Thank you so much, Bro. Ted, for sharing your enthusiasm for the fraternity, for signing my petition, and for everything you have done for my family and me over the years. I love you brother.

I petitioned Stokesdale Lodge No. 428 in May, 1997. Most Worshipful Bill Simpson, (1996), Worshipful Ray Comer, and Worshipful Clyde Howerton served as my primary mentors, along with my coach, Worshipful Jesse Joyce. They each taught me something different about the brotherhood – the mystery, the tradition, the ritual, the need for patience and humility, and the importance of communication. I thank each of them for the roles they played in helping me become the man and Mason I am today.

I want to thank my family: Sharon, Graham, and Brantleigh. My desire to be a better husband and father inspired me to become a Freemason and to study the deeper aspects of the Craft. Thank you for your selfless sacrifices as I spent countless hours traveling, studying, reading, writing, editing, teaching, and leading my beloved fraternity. I could not have made this journey without you and I am so appreciative of your encouragement and support over the years. I love you all so much and I am deeply grateful to have you in my life.

Finally, to my co-author, brother, and friend, Ben Wallace, thank you for giving me an opportunity to be part of this project. I appreciate your esoteric wisdom, your spiritual insight, and your extraordinary patience as we've gone through this journey together. I love you brother!

With warm fraternal love,
Shaun

Table of Contents

Foreword

In addition to the excitement of beginning a new journey, I will never forget the warm and comforting feelings that overcame me the night I was initiated into the mysteries of Freemasonry in Potomac Lodge No. 5. I will also never forget the promise Freemasonry made to me 25 years ago to help me transform myself into a better human being. Regrettably and for the longest time, I was unable to comprehend what I had experienced, nor was I given proper instruction to help me decipher and build on it. Providentially, as the authors of this book would put it, my attentive ear met, a few years later, the instructive tongue of a dear (recently departed) Brother who pointed me in the direction of Freemasonry's esoteric nature. How fortunate was I! Since then, and for the past 20 years, I have made Masonic Education my cause in our Noble Craft and it was the centerpiece of my Trestle Board when I had the honor and privilege to serve as Grand Master of our Nation's Capital.

As mentioned by the authors, Masonic Education has regrettably been reduced to teaching protocol, traditions, and catechism while ignoring the esoteric essence of the ritual. Esoteric, from the Latin word esotero originally esoterikos in Greek, simply means secret within or hidden within. Freemasonry's essence is esoteric and is universally defined as a peculiar system of morality, veiled in allegory, and illustrated by symbols designed to help a person improve. The primary purpose of Masonic Education should therefore be to assist initiates in delving deeper into the allegories and symbols at the core of Freemasonry's rituals. In doing so, they are encouraged to each draw their own designs to become a "better person", i.e., a free builder. You can therefore imagine my joy when I learned about the Middle Chamber Program that the Grand Lodge of North Carolina institutionalized in 2017 and overseen by Grand Master Shaun Bradshaw. Having a structured and rigorous program of Masonic Education that points to practical applications of Freemasonry's esoteric teachings is of utmost importance. Without it, Freemasonry's potential may become dormant and its promise unfulfilled.

I must admit I was thrilled to read the draft of *A Path to Providence: The Creation of the Middle Chamber Program.* Brothers Shaun Bradshaw and Ben Wallace are determined to spread the light by sharing this program and experience with seekers in all jurisdictions. Margaret Fuller, an American journalist, critic, and women's rights advocate of the 19th Century said: "If you have knowledge, let others light their candles in it." How Masonic! The hidden meanings of Freemasonry's teachings point to the esoteric connection between Relief, Charity, and Freedom. Indeed, giving back is an essential ingredient in the secret Masonic formula for one to achieve true freedom. Our Brothers here, have generously shared their worthy talents.

I pray and hope when you finish reading this book, you feel more energized and committed to learning more about the North Carolina experiment in Masonic Education and help take it even further to greater heights. We need a focused effort and sustained commitment towards Masonic Education across the country because Freemasonry has a "rendezvous with destiny" in 2026.

Five short years from now, America, the Great Experiment in human governance, will mark its 250th Anniversary. Whence came ye America? Whence came ye as Entered Apprentice Masons?

With the aid of Providence in 1776, the Founding Fathers of the United States launched an incredible experiment by placing the core of governance with the people, not the government. Freemasonry's legacy in connection to this Great Experiment has been its capability and readiness to graduate citizens of this republic who are committed to and equipped for self-governance, community building, democratic institutions, and the spread of enlightened freedom.

Will Freemasonry rise to the challenge now as it did in the past? Given current conditions in the United States, we will need the concerted efforts of many free, enlightened, and engaged citizens who are committed to build more beautiful, stronger, and wiser selves and communities. I am confident the Middle Chamber Program will be a powerful tool in the noble effort to arouse the spirit and mind, to awaken the creative energies of large numbers of initiates by connecting them to the Freemasonry's hidden mysteries. Welcome to the Mystic Tie!

AKRAM R. ELIAS
2008 Grand Master
Grand Lodge of Free and Accepted Masons
March, 2021   Washington, D.C.

Special Note on Titles

Freemasons love titles. Brother, Worshipful, Right Worshipful, Most Worshipful, Illustrious, Illustrious Sir, Sir Knight... we could go on. Within the fraternity, each title has meaning and, beyond paying due homage to the brother's rank, may also express context for the organization or timeframe being discussed.

To some of our brethren, not using the correct title is considered a slight, while other brethren believe using these titles may do nothing more than stroke a brother's ego. Regardless of where you fall on the spectrum, it's important we bring special attention to our use of titles in this work.

Most Worshipful Brother Shaun Bradshaw played an imminent role in this story, but when it began, his proper title was Right Worshipful, as he was an elected member of the Grand Line of North Carolina but had not been elevated to the rank of Grand Master. As the story unfolds however, his rank and title changed. In addition to Bro. Bradshaw, other members of the Craft whose titles changed also come into play.

To minimize confusion, the authors have chosen to refer to any member of the fraternity with the more general title "Brother," except where using a specific title may be necessary for the context of the story. This is not an intended slight toward any of our brethren, but to enhance the reader's ability to digest the information without getting caught up in the titles.

Preface

Providence, Synchronicity, God's Plan. Whatever you call it, the Universe brings people, ideas, and circumstances together for great purpose. For the authors, this story is a perfect example of Providence working in our lives toward some great purpose.

For years, the leadership in the Grand Lodge of North Carolina has placed significant emphasis on the role of education to improve the administration, finances, and culture (tone) of the meetings in its subordinate lodges. The Wilkerson College Program came first, an intensive set of leadership workshops open to Deacons of the lodges, spanning three weekends with a curriculum covering everything from the history of the fraternity, to preparing budgets for the lodges, to planning a year's worth of Masonic events. Next came the Davie Leadership Academy. These workshops were open to any Master Mason and covered a variety of topics relevant to our members. The most recent addition to the list of outstanding educational initiatives is the Middle Chamber Program.

Each of these educational programs are wonderful and rightly deserve attention, but this book's focus is the Middle Chamber Program. Multiple elements make this program unique. It's an in-person, instructor led course that focuses on the esoteric aspects of the Craft's rituals and symbols. This program is also fully sanctioned by the leadership of the Grand Lodge of North Carolina and administered through the Committee on Masonic Education.

In preparing this story, it's worthwhile to understand how this book originated. For those involved in developing the idea, the curriculum, the schedule, and the logistics of the program, the story wrote itself. As roadblocks emerged, Providence provided an alternate route. Seeing the enthusiasm from the brethren who have attended the classes, as well as the excitement of brethren outside the Jurisdiction who have learned about this program, it seemed natural to document, not just what the program is and how other Grand

Lodges can implement something similar for themselves, but equally important to convey how it came to be. That's the purpose of this book: to tell this story because it's important to share how Providence works in our lives and how we are called to duty to act through our own free will when aligned with the will of Deity.

We hope our brethren will find inspiration in this book to pursue their esoteric journey through the Craft and expand those learnings into similar programs within their lodges and Grand Jurisdictions throughout the United States. As Bro. Shaun is fond of saying, "Each one, teach one." At some point in the near future, it's our sincere hope every lodge will have at least one brother who's on the path to understand the esoteric workings of the degrees so when a new member joins the lodge, one who has an interest and desire to learn that aspect of our Craft, that brother can take him by the hand and lead him on this wonderful journey.

Sincerely & Fraternally,

P. Shaun Bradshaw & Benjamin G. Wallace

THE "STORY BEHIND THE STORY"

— From Bro. Shaun's Perspective —

After a couple of successful years with the Middle Chamber program, Brother Ben approached me in 2019 to suggest I write a book explaining the program's origins. I knew this was more Bro. Ben's story to tell and deferred the project to him, especially since I expected to be busy as Grand Master in 2020. Bro. Ben willingly accepted the project and I agreed to review and edit the book, which he affectionately dubbed "Bradshaw's Folly." Fast forward several months when Providence provided a new path.

On October 19, 2019, a number of Middle Chamber graduates gathered at the Masonic Home for Children in Oxford, NC to participate in a capstone class we called the Inner Chamber. During a special, esoteric exercise I had one of the most profound experiences of my life, which led me to understand the necessity of my deeper involvement in this project. Emotion wells up as I write those words, recalling the moment when I stood alone in an incense-filled, candle lit lodge room and heard unspoken words urging me to take a direct role with this book. A few days later, I approached Bro. Ben to share my experience. I explained that during the esoteric exercise it became clear I had to take an active part in the project by contributing as a co-author, not simply as an editor. I asked if I could, "add my voice to the story" he had drafted.

Elated by the news, Bro. Ben readily agreed!

Over the years, I have come to recognize Providence's hand in my life, and each time it has led me to a better understanding of myself and my journey in this world. I've never considered myself an author or someone with a book in me, and how important my contributions to this work are remain to be seen. But when Providence speaks, I've learned to listen and follow the path it's revealed to me.

Chapter One

The Tabernacle

*After Moses had conducted the children of Israel through the Red Sea, into the wilderness, when pursued by Pharaoh and his host, he there, by divine command, erected a **tabernacle** due East and West, in order to perpetuate the remembrance of that mighty East wind, by which their Miraculous deliverance was wrought, and also to receive the rays of the rising sun.*

—Bahnson, North Carolina Lodge Manual

The Ancient Landmarks of Freemasonry are the rock-solid foundation the fraternity has been built upon and provides the necessary stability to maintain its core meaning and teachings for centuries of its existence. Yet, other features of this great institution have shifted and evolved, allowing it to stay relevant in the societies and cultures blessed with its presence. Just as the tabernacle, erected by Moses, was the model for King Solomon's Temple, so has the edifice - the fraternity's outward focus - changed with time. But despite these changes, the essence of the Craft - its moral, spiritual, and esoteric foundation - has remained the same.

We are an ancient institution. Study of it requires a long view of our history, even if much of the early record is lost in the ravages of time. Fortunately, one element of recent history in the United States has been diligently tracked by the Masonic Service Association of

North America (MSANA), through our membership statistics. While the membership numbers only provide a single dimension of our Craft, it is an interesting view.

The MSANA provides membership data on its website as reported by the various Grand Lodges in the United States beginning in 1924 when we boasted a total of 3,077,161 Freemasons in America.

It is no surprise that the Great Depression drove a sharp membership decline in the fraternity throughout the United States and the world. This sharp decline was not our first, nor would it be our last major shift in membership. As ocean tides ebb and flow, so did our membership after WWII ended. In a tsunami-like rise, Freemasonry's rolls increased from 2,896,343 in the United States in 1945 to 4,103,161 in 1959, an almost 42% increase in 14 years.

Today, we hardly recognize how difficult these times were for our country. Both the Great Depression and the war required a true national effort. The Americans who served in the military, as well as those who worked on the home front, bonded by difficulties that earned them the title The Greatest Generation.

Fueled by hardships faced in their youth and throughout the war, the Greatest Generation became fraternal joiners. This drove much of the growth in Freemasonry. All fraternal institutions flourished in the immediate postwar era, but none more than Masonry. The Freemasons of the time may have believed this membership explosion would last forever, but the luxury of hindsight shows it was a bubble. From the high-water mark of 1959, Masonic rolls across the United States began a steady decline, falling below 3 million members in 1984, then shrinking to fewer than 2 million members in 1998. The most recent data available is from 2017 and shows membership down to only 1,076,626 members. Where this trend levels off is greatly debated across all Grand Jurisdictions.

The influx of fraternal members brought two major problems. The first was dilution of understanding. As membership grew, those who understood the deeper meanings of the rituals and symbols had difficulty sharing their knowledge across the vast ranks of new members. With so many men joining and too little time allotted to absorb the lessons as lodges pushed them through the degrees, the new members had fewer opportunities to engage in the spiritual aspects of the Craft. Eventually, those members who were more interested in continuing the fraternal relationships established during the war gained more influence than those seeking deeper truths and these "truth seekers" were pushed to the fraternity's outskirts.

The second major problem revolved around money. The membership increases allowed lodges and Grand Lodges to keep dues and per capita artificially low. Initiation fees and dues once equaled two to three weeks of wages, but increased membership rolls allowed lodges to maintain the same level of dues while increasing funding in their investments, charities, and buildings and continuing to provide a positive experience for those who were active. Now, with the drastic drop in membership numbers over the last four decades, the money has dried up. Members who joined at the height of fraternal membership became accustomed to low dues and for years were unwilling to increase them to meet the financial burdens of their lodges and Grand Lodges. Instead, they opted to draw from investments to cover the difference. Many ignored much needed maintenance and repairs to the buildings of which they were so proud, causing them to become an albatross around the necks of the current members.

Various Grand Lodges across the United States are approaching this perceived membership emergency and *very real* money shortfall in different ways. Some have made joining cheaper and easier in hopes membership levels return to those of years ago. One-day classes, reduced or eliminated catechisms, and marketing schemes are one approach. Other Grand Lodges believe if they focus on member quality and perceived value, the money will follow. Their thought is, members will readily pay more if they find true value in their Masonic experience.

The only certainty seems to be this: the institution will be different when we get to the far side of this crisis.

REALITY VS. POSSIBILITY

The Reality vs. Possibility Matrix is a popular method of depicting organizational transformation. This model shows how organizations survive through continuous and managed transformation. The typical path for most organizations is shown in **Figure 1**.

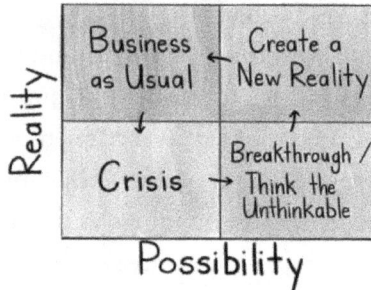

Figure 1

Here you see organizations begin in a state of Business as Usual. Over time, their product, delivery model, leadership, and/or employees become stagnant or an outside force intervenes to cause a Crisis. At this point an organization has two choices. Transform and grow through the crisis or hold steady and face potential demise. Organizations that choose to Think the Unthinkable and change to meet new challenges, find themselves having Created a New Reality.

Over time, this new reality becomes the next Business as Usual. The key to supporting organizational survival and success, is seeking ways to avoid the Crisis by continuously encouraging Breakthrough Thinking.

Freemasonry in the United States now faces a similar challenge. The crisis of dwindling numbers forces leaders to either consider breakthrough ideas or face continued drops in revenue and members. As many in the fraternity seek ideas to gain more members, the true leaders should ask, is this goal Breakthrough Thinking or merely a return to Business as Usual?

In many ways we still live our grandfathers' Freemasonry, pre-dominantly manifested as a form of the Craft focused almost exclusively on charities and public fundraisers necessary to maintain solvency. Members parrot ritual without a deeper understanding of the spoken words, attend business meetings aimed at keeping the lights on instead of spreading fraternal light, and maintain social bonds that lean more toward cultural exclusion versus tolerance and inclusion.

Until recently, the Craft has changed little, despite the world changing around it. We have gutted it out while holding on by our fraternal fingernails in a desperate attempt to maintain the status quo. Our buildings have been neglected to the point of crisis as we've stubbornly kept our initiation fees and annual dues as low as possible. Outsiders who read this may look on in bewilderment as the brethren who understand it will sadly agree.

What will become of the fraternity, in relation to its buildings and money, is not the focus of this book. However, understanding these problems are necessary to set the stage for the story.

As mentioned earlier, the men flooding into the fraternity during those glory years of ever-increasing numbers, joined primarily for fraternal reasons. Few, if any, held interest in the esoteric nature of the Craft, instead choosing to create opportunities to socialize with each other. Life experiences taught them people must work together for common causes, but subsequent generations have not subscribed to that same sense of fraternalism as those who came of age in The Greatest Generation.

The counterculture of the 1960s further diminished the joiner attitude as socially beneficial or even acceptable. Baby boomers did not support the golden age of fraternalism their parents had launched. All these combined to push the spiritual and philosophical aspects of the Craft from the lodge, or at least into the metaphorical broom closet.

While the basic moral lessons illustrated in our rituals give members pragmatic ways to consider their duties in this world, most fraternally-minded brethren have no interest in the deeper and richer lessons our degrees offer under the veil of *allegory* and *symbolism*. To be clear, we're not implying this is wrong. This is simply how the fraternity evolved… the way the situation developed.

As more fraternally-minded brethren rose into leadership offices in local lodges and eventually in Grand Lodges, nearly all the positions were filled by this group who emphasized the fraternity's social benefits and charities. Now, when a new Mason seeks deeper meanings beyond the superficial explanations given in the degrees, the fraternally-focused leadership does not know where to direct him. They didn't join to learn the esoteric interpretations of the degrees and didn't understand that aspect of the Craft. Worse yet, many considered anything esoteric to be antithetical to *their* fraternity's core and not only avoided these topics, but actively opposed them. The human ego drove lodge leaders to tell young seekers, "We don't talk about that stuff here," or "You'll learn those lessons when you're ready." Sometimes the leaders didn't believe there were deeper meanings than the surface explanations. Or perhaps they felt something deeper was there, but shrugged it off not knowing what *it* was.

For several generations, men looking for true enlightenment through Masonic Philosophy discovered they were in the wrong place. Some remained card-carrying members but did not attend meetings. Others drifted away. Yet, as the Merovingian said in *Matrix Reloaded*, "You see, there is only one constant, one universal, it is the only real truth: Causality. Action. Reaction. Cause and effect."

A PERSISTENT SEARCH FOR DEEPER TRUTHS

— From Bro. Ben's Perspective —

I joined the lodge after reading *The Da Vinci Code* by Dan Brown. The ideas presented in the book drove me to seek deeper meanings of the Craft and I suspected they were hidden below the surface level of teaching. When I heard the instruction given in the Northeast corner, that the lessons of the degrees were "veiled in allegory and illustrated by symbols," I knew my assumptions were correct. After being assigned a coach to learn my catechism, I recall asking him when we would get to the deeper stuff. I was told the memorization of the catechism *was* the deeper stuff. Further inquiries led me to understand my coach simply didn't know the allegorical and symbolical meanings beyond the surface explanations. I then began asking the same question of Masters, Past Masters, and anyone in a position of perceived power. I realized very few, if any, truly understood the Craft at a deeper level. Yet my intuition led me to keep searching. I joined appendant bodies, read books, scoured the internet, and met Masonic philosophers from across the nation. Over time, I developed the right contacts and discovered various paths leading toward a better understanding of the esoteric lessons given in the Craft Degrees.

While I was steadfast in my search for spiritual and philosophical aspects of the degrees, the sobering truth is many brethren who join for similar reasons leave before finding a brother or group who can mentor them. Our hope is this book, and the program it promotes, will help future brethren find what they seek by giving other lodges and Grand Jurisdictions a model to establish an esoteric education program.

With the fraternal-minded leadership firmly entrenched, the Craft drew further away from the deeper explanations of its degrees. Eventually, the brethren with a more philosophical approach to Freemasonry, the predecessors of the fraternal high tide, died off. With them went much wisdom. Only in small circles, and by individual study, did a few brethren hold on to the profound Truths of the ritual. We have come to call these men Knowers, but lodges rarely welcomed their opinions so their teachings and understandings largely remained undiscovered. Every adept understands you cannot impose lessons on those who are not ready to receive them. As the culture in lodges tilted away from the deeper Truths and Meanings of the degrees, the adepts withdrew to the fringes with their knowledge and wisdom. As the fraternal bubble expanded, the Knowers were pushed further from the center and nearly lost.

Yet, throughout this period, the ritual remained substantially the same, untouched by well-intended reformers and innovators. Increasing membership required better organizational skills, so as Grand Lodges grew, they became more bureaucratic and administratively proficient. In a strange, almost Providential twist of fate, Grand Lodges developed a formalized system of ritual keepers. Called different things in different states, the purpose of these committees and boards is to guard the ritual and set it into a nearly unchangeable form. This is a relatively new innovation in the Craft. A study of our history shows a dizzying array of rituals used, modified, changed, and amalgamated. Local lodges often used different variations of the ritual. In North Carolina our Grand Lodge used a system of district lecturers from at least 1837. These were circuit-riding lecturers initially paid by the lodges—and later by the Grand Lodge—who empowered them to teach the work over large geographic areas. To make this system more effective, the Grand Lodge of North Carolina formed the Board of Custodians in 1903. This replaced the older system of ritual keepers and directly solidified the ritual in a static and unchanging form, resulting in no significant ritual modifications in North Carolina for at least 180 years.

This single action by the Grand Lodge may have saved the spirit of Freemasonry. The ritual is key to preserving Freemasonry's veiled and allegorical lessons and if Providence could not save the Craft from being overtaken by a fraternal swarm, at least it preserved the rock-solid foundation of what we truly are until the right time to resurrect the core truth of the degrees.

Today, we have an interesting, but not totally new situation. While the leaders and administrators of Freemasonry struggle to decide what to do about falling membership and decreasing revenues, a small but passionate group of brethren have noticed a tidal shift. They recognize the fraternity is poised for its next evolution.

If you only observed the short term, it may appear the Grand Architect had sucked all the esoteric knowledge of the Craft into his mighty lungs where he intended to keep it just beyond our reach... forever. However, taking the long view of history, one can see this situation for its reality. In Freemasonry's ever-changing tidal cycles, the fraternal bubble is now ebbing. As those waters retreat, we may be surprised to discover what has been hidden below the surface. With preserved ritual in our hands and the tabernacle of fraternal-minded dominance withdrawing, a foundation has been set for the return of the third Principal Tenet of Masonry: Truth. Of course, the spiritual and philosophical nature of the ritual were never truly lost. They simply faded into the background until members could understand and appreciate them again.

It is time to build a more permanent structure, to move from the tabernacle to the temple, and give our initiates a place wherein they may learn and contemplate the esoteric foundation of our Craft.

Chapter Two

Mt. Moriah

This vast fabric [of the Temple] was founded in the fourth year of the reign of King Solomon, during the second month of the sacred year, on the hill of Mt. Moriah, near the place where Abraham was about to offer up Isaac, and where David met and appeased the destroying angel.

—Bahnson, North Carolina Lodge Manual

It would be impossible to tell the story of the Middle Chamber Program without an explanation of its foundation, which lies in the Traditional Observant movement in general and Sophia Lodge No. 767, specifically.

For those who may be unfamiliar with the Traditional Observant (or T.O). movement, this simply refers to a set of lodge practices that are intended to elevate the experience of the members when attending their regular lodge meetings. With few exceptions, the Traditional Observant movement has successfully spread through nearly every jurisdiction in the United States and differs from the typical lodge experience in a number of ways. Observant lodges commonly feature a higher dues structure, require formal dress for members and visitors, accentuate their meetings with incense, candles and music, and enjoy formalized lodge meals (called Harmonies), which include Masonic toasts and songs. Also, Observant lodges commit to ritual excellence and emphasize Keeping the Light, not just keeping the lights on.

The Traditional Observant movement began in the United States in the 1990's. In 2001, The Masonic Restoration Foundation (MRF) was formed to support lodges who were working this style of Masonry. They began hosting a yearly symposium where brethren from around the country came together to share their practices and encourage others to experiment with similar changes to enhance their own lodge experience. By sharing the vision of an improved lodge experience, the MRF quickened what was only a conceptual idea for many Masons and helped guide them through the process in their own jurisdictions. In short, it took what were a disparate scattering of lodge working styles, and through inspiration and teaching, kindled a flame that grew into a movement.

Most Observant lodges will follow the basic concepts above in an effort to stimulate the five senses described in the ritual, which allows for a unique lodge experience, compared to the practices of most lodges in the United States today. It should be noted that while Observant Masonry's method of presentation is completely different from other lodges, the forms and ceremonies used are the same as any other lodge in their jurisdiction.

The presentation method may be considered its outer wrapping, but, like our rituals, there are deeper layers of purpose to many Observant lodges. One layer includes a greater appreciation for the depth of wisdom given in the degrees. We are told very early in our initiation ceremony that Freemasonry is "a beautiful system of morality, *veiled in allegory* and *illustrated by symbols.*" The Observant Mason seeks to explore this allegory and symbolism, to unwrap the outer layers of meaning, to discover the true essence awaiting him who seeks. Not every Traditional Observance lodge or Observant Mason pursues this depth of understanding, but the Observant Model often attracts the type of brethren who do.

In 2010 Bro. Andrew Hammer published the book *Observing the Craft.* It was the first work, and remains the best, on what he explicitly refers to as Observant Masonry[1]. This book is an inspirational call to arms for all who yearn for the reverence this style of lodge offers its practitioners.

During this same period, Enlightenment Lodge No. 198 was almost certainly the most visible and vibrant Traditional Observance lodge in the country due to members who had larger than life personalities, a knack for writing, and a passion to share and grow their experience at Enlightenment Lodge. They were a bright star within the T.O. community. The internet buzzed with excitement over this renewed interest in old ways and Enlightenment Lodge was front and center of the movement.

MASONIC RESTORATION FOUNDATION MISSION

"The many Lodges, Grand Lodges, and individual Masons who support the work of the MRF believe that when lodges practice Masonry as a transformative art, they become a part of the true heritage of Freemasonry that has been established over hundreds of years and has been energized through hundreds of rituals, which have been repeated thousands of times. Such places have spectacular reserves of energy, all focused on a single, foundational hope—the improvement in the individual man and Mason."

Bro. Ben Wallace had an opportunity to visit Enlightenment Lodge No. 198 in Colorado Springs when it was at its height of glory and, having read Bro. Hammer's intoxicating message of hope for the Craft, he helped form a small group of North Carolina Masons to consider forming a similar lodge in North Carolina.

In April of 2013 Bro. Hammer was invited to visit Wilkerson College Lodge No. 760 as part of its National Level Speaker program.

---

[1] Bro. Hammer insists that the word "Traditional" should not be used with the concept of this style of Freemasonry, asking "What Tradition are you referring to?" We have used the terms Traditional Observant, Traditional Observance, and Observant interchangeably due to their frequent and common use in the vernacular.

This is an educational themed lodge that was an outgrowth of North Carolina's groundbreaking leadership and management course called Wilkerson College. Bro. Hammer is a fiery orator and, on this day, he inspired many. This meeting, and the subsequent Harmony, sparked the flame that moved the idea of a North Carolina Traditional Observance lodge from concept to reality.

The creation of Sophia Lodge No. 767 is an inspirational story in itself and we hope it will be told someday in full. For our purposes however, it's sufficient to point out that the idea envisioned by its charter members was brought into manifestation and continues to be an inspiration to all who experience it.

Like all lodges, Sophia has its own personality and culture. The founding members of *any* lodge set the tone for how that lodge will look and feel. Having been created on the Traditional Observant model, Sophia has an egregore, which especially promotes education in the philosophical and spiritual aspects of the Craft. Not every Traditional Observance lodge has this foundation, but Sophia has since its beginning and continues to do so. Bro. Bradshaw has noted, while Sophia Lodge expounds the ideals of a Traditional Observance lodge, it is more than a "TO Lodge." It is difficult to put into words and must be felt to be understood. Something magical happens when we enter the lodge. It's as though something spiritual descends upon us as we meet within.

GRAHAM'S STORY

In October 2018, Bro. Bradshaw's son, Graham, asked him how to become a Mason. Graham saw the men his father associated with, knew of the fraternity, and believed going through the initiatic experience would help him become a better man.

At the time, Bro. Bradshaw belonged to four lodges, each with its own culture and emphasis on the social, charitable, educational, and esoteric aspects of the Craft. Based on his father's descriptions of each lodge, Graham chose to join Bro. Bradshaw's home lodge, Stokesdale No. 428.

Stokesdale is a rural lodge with a less formal culture and, while the members are friendly, charitable, and do excellent degree work, Bro. Bradshaw believed Graham should experience at least one degree in a more esoteric setting. Bro. Bradshaw discussed this with Graham and together they decided that Graham would be initiated in his home lodge but take his Fellow Craft degree at Sophia Lodge, then be raised a Master Mason back at Stokesdale.

Each of the degrees were wonderfully executed in their own right, but after completing all the degrees, Bro. Graham spoke to his father about his experience in each of the lodges. He noted that while he always felt comfortable at Stokesdale Lodge, the most enlightening experience from all of his degree work was at Sophia.

Sophia Lodge employs the use of a Chamber of Reflection prior to each degree. The Chamber is simply adorned: a candle, a mirror, and a few symbolic items, for the candidate's contemplation. According to Graham, the time he spent in the Chamber of Reflection was the most transformative experience of any of his degree work and greatly enhanced the lessons of the degrees.

Sophia Lodge strives to bring this concept to all its work: a transformative, ritualistic experience.

Keeping with its core concepts, Sophia's officers developed an in-house program in 2015 to teach the members and new initiates more about the degrees. The curriculum focused on the esoteric lessons of the ritual. The program's success birthed something much grander, although we didn't realize it at the time.

One of the many things Providence provided for, on this ever-evolving idea that became the Middle Chamber Program, was Sophia had several Grand Line officers as charter members. This resulted in many of them attending the internal classes and being exposed to the ideas espoused by the lodge culture. Prior to serving as Grand Master of Masons in North Carolina in 2015, Most Worshipful Doug Caudle had participated in the classes at Sophia. When presented with the idea to expand those classes and make them available to the entire Grand Jurisdiction, he granted permission without hesitation.

One cannot understate the risk this involved for Grand Master Caudle and the Grand Lodge. For many prudent reasons, Grand Lodges are remiss to allow this type instruction to be given in a jurisdiction-wide and completely sanctioned vehicle. There are many ways this could go wrong. Concerns of interpretation, context, presentation, egos, and more must be considered. The fact that Bro. Caudle and other Grand Line officers had been exposed to the Sophia version of these lectures allayed many potential concerns. The risks were also minimized because of the trusted relationship with the instructors, as well as understanding there was a pent-up demand for this type of instruction throughout the state.

It still took enormous courage and confidence to allow the idea to proceed. It is easy to take the safe route and politely decline such a groundbreaking program, but our leadership met the call. Bravery and vision are critical to facilitate change. No one has significantly impacted the world by playing it safe and the Grand Lodge of North Carolina was (and continues to be) blessed with brave and visionary leadership throughout the establishment of what came to be known as *The Middle Chamber Program*.

GRAND LODGE LEADERSHIP CONTINUITY AND TRUST

Each Grand Jurisdiction in the United States has its own, somewhat unique, method of appointing and electing its Grand Lodge officers. Some Grand Jurisdictions allow nominations from the floor for Grand Wardens, Deputy Grand Master, and Grand Master, while others permit no nominations or electioneering for these high offices. In North Carolina, once the Deputy Grand Master is elected Grand Master, tradition dictates he appoint the new Junior Grand Steward who serves in a five-year progressive appointed line before entering the elected line as Grand Junior Warden. By the time the Deputy Grand Master is elected Grand Master he has served eight years as a Grand Lodge officer and has had an opportunity to get to know, and work with, each of the other Grand Lodge officers on a personal, professional, and Masonic level.

Because the Grand Lodge officers are appointed and do not campaign against each other, there's a greater sense of camaraderie amongst them and a greater likelihood each of them will support the long term/strategic goals of their predecessors and to the benefit of the Grand Jurisdiction. In fact, most Deputy Grand Masters seek potential appointees who have the skills, experience, and personalities to complement the other Grand Line officers. This means they tend to get along and don't (generally) work at a cross purposes to each other, thus ensuring leadership continuity that's based more on ability than popularity.

In relation to the creation and promotion of the Middle Chamber Program, this system of Grand Lodge leadership sets up well because the program isn't viewed as any particular Grand Master's program, but rather a program that has continuous support across many Grand Masters.

Sophia was the first Traditional Observance lodge in North Carolina and, at the time these events unfolded, it was new and quite the curiosity. Anything that's new and different attracts attention and in our Grand Jurisdiction, all eyes scrutinized us. Chatter amongst some North Carolina Masons rumored this new type of lodge was trying to change "the way we practice Freemasonry," the concern being this new program may demand members interpret *their* Masonry in a new way. In the end, we won over most naysayers by offering a superb lodge experience while keeping our unique approach to Freemasonry in house. We were careful not to criticize other lodges or profess we "did Masonry right the way" and everyone else "did it wrong". Eventually our brethren were either won over by our approach, or simply left us to our own ways. But early on, the jury was still out.

Fortunately, the Grand Lodge recognized the program's potential and trusted us to develop the "in house" lecture series into something we could share with a wider audience. Convinced an appetite existed for more esoteric, philosophical, and spiritual Masonic information across the state, we began work on a lecture series specifically focused on those aspects of the degrees, all with permission from the Grand Lodge.

Chapter Three

Designs Upon the Trestle-Board

By the trestle-board we are also reminded, that as the operative workman erects his temporal building agreeably to the rules and designs laid down by the Master on the trestle-board, so should we, both operative and speculative, endeavor to erect our spiritual building agreeably to the rules and designs laid down by the Supreme Architect of the Universe, in the great books of nature and revelation, which are our spiritual, moral, and Masonic trestle-board.

—Bahnson, North Carolina Lodge Manual

Before the workmen were employed, before the foundation's footings were dug, even before the materials were gathered, the designs of the Temple had to be envisioned and committed to the trestle-board. In the case of the Middle Chamber Program, Sophia Lodge's esoteric lectures served as the initial plans upon which its designs could be adorned and expanded.

The "Allegory and Symbolism" lectures, as they came to be known, proved extremely popular. Technically, they operated under the banner of the Grand Lodge Committee on Masonic Education, however, they functioned mostly as an autonomous entity, with the team who created the program maintaining responsibility for executing it.

The original three-hour lectures consisted of four instructional blocks consisting of opening dialog, followed by a section on each of the three degrees (Entered Apprentice, Fellow Craft, and Master Mason). In addition to the instructional blocks, time was set aside for a brief introduction, some administrative points, a couple of breaks, and questions and answers. For those interested in the Craft's esoteric nature, the lectures delivered, but given the limitations in time allotted for instruction, they could only scratch the surface of most topics.

ALLEGORY & SYMBOLISM LECTURES - A BRIEF OUTLINE

These early lectures covered the Craft's basic premises as described in Wilmshurst's *The Meaning of Masonry* and MacNulty's *The Way of the Craftsman*, while delivered in a manner to make these concepts accessible to most brethren. A general discussion on symbolism paved the way to discuss the Lodge as a model of the Self and psyche. The idea of the Material, Psychological, and Spiritual aspects of man were conveyed through both explanation and stories. Instructors emphasized the need for aspirants to relentlessly pursue knowledge to free their minds from preconceived notions. Finally, the Hiramic legend was shown as a parable of the great sacrifice true initiates must make to be raised as better versions of themselves.

The general outline from these lectures served as an early trestle-board, or design, for what is now taught in the Middle Chamber program and included brief discussions on the following topics and symbols:

Introduction

- The lesson of the Northeast Corner
- The Western Mystery Tradition and comparisons to Freemasonry
- Masonic History
- Masonic Philosophy

Entered Apprentice Degree

- Primary aspects of the degree
- Key symbols of the degree
  - The Lights
  - The Square and Compasses
  - The Apron
  - The Demand
  - The Northeast Corner
  - The Working Tools
- Main points of the Lecture

Fellow Craft Degree

- Primary aspects of the Degree
- Key symbols of the Lecture
  - The Columns
  - The 3, 5, 7 Steps
  - The Ephramites story
  - The Middle Chamber

Master Mason Degree

- Brief review of the First Section
- Key symbols and allegories of the Second Section
  - The Officers
  - The Empty Chair
  - The Entrance
  - The Prayer
  - The Ruffians
  - The Assault
  - The Rubbish of the Temple
  - The Brow of the Hill
  - The Search
  - The Fellow Crafts
  - The Raising
- Discuss main points of the lecture

To minimize organizational red tape and reduce Grand Lodge overhead, the lectures were provided free to any Master Mason with no pre-registration required. Marketing consisted of a few flyers and lodge mailings and the team designed the lectures for a narrow audience, one they believed would be most open to their esoteric nature.

North Carolina is a short yet wide state, running approximately 500 miles from east to west and 150 miles from north to south. The team designed the schedule by dividing the state into four relatively equal sections with the lectures being given in each area. By dividing the state this way, the hope was to attract interested members while reducing their travel burden. Making it more convenient for the attendees, however, required the instructors to spend more time on the road and facilitate more sessions, but all the initial team members were so passionate about this program that they eagerly drove hours to share it with brethren across the state.

As word spread about the lectures, they became increasingly popular. The initial concern was we'd pour significant time and effort into a program that few brethren would be interested in. Perhaps the expenditure in man hours and fuel could be better used in other areas? Yet, the class sizes were consistently larger than expected. The next concern was the program's sustainability. Would interest fade once the first group of Masons cycled through the lectures? This turned out not to be the case. There was significant pent-up demand for these types of lectures and as word spread among the brethren, attendance grew. In fact, the lectures proved so popular and informative, many brethren would come again (often bringing a friend with them) to hear the lectures a second and third time in hopes of gaining more insight about the degrees.

This was wholly unexpected and led us to explore the cause of this seeming enigma. As we alluded to earlier, the spiritual and philosophical aspects of the Craft had been (consequently, not purposefully) suppressed for decades. It was almost unthinkable that anything other than a smattering of brethren would be interested in these lectures simply because so few had ever been exposed to Freemasonry's esoteric philosophy. Yet here they were; attending in surprising numbers. Our fears that the initial excitement would quickly wear off proved to be completely unfounded. Apparently, a great number of interested brethren had been there all along, right under our noses.

While some of the participants were new to the Craft, most had been members for years, harboring a yearning for the deeper meanings of the ritual and waiting for someone to share it with them. We can only guess at how many brethren drifted away from lodges over the years, not having found what they sought from the fraternity. Yet in these classes, were the brethren who had toughed it out, their hope of a program like this ending in fruition.

As we assessed the unexpected interest in the lectures, we set our sights on what else this program could develop into. Perhaps it was possible to create an actual initiatic school of sorts. Could this be possible?

All of us who were involved in developing The Middle Chamber Program believe that Freemasonry at its core, has the bones of a classical Western Mystery system. Whether it was set up this way in the strictly operative days, or grafted onto the old operative system by early speculative members or founders of the early Grand Lodges, or Freemasonry simply grew into it through accident and Providence, will never likely be solved. But for those with eyes to see, it has the hallmarks of an old mystery school. Progressive art? Check. Three-tiered, neo-platonic structure? Check. Structured ritual? Check. Conducted in a sacred space? Check. System of proficiency to pass to the next level? Check. Outer system of teachings? Check. Deeper level of teachings hidden by allegory and symbolism? Absolutely. Our ritual specifically tells us this. All the elements were right in front of us, we simply weren't using them as intended. Walter Leslie Wilmshurst reminds us that "In all the schools of the Mysteries, as well as in all the great religions of the world, the attainment of the spiritual goal...is enacted or taught under the veil of a tragic episode analogous to that of our third degree; and in each there is a Master whose death the aspirant is instructed he must imitate in his own person.[2]"

The problem is, if Freemasonry was based on an ancient mystery tradition, it had lost its way somewhere along the level of time. It's easy enough to find examples of Dr. Mackey (19th century), Thomas Smith Webb (19th century) or even William Preston (late 18th century) complaining about brethren who misunderstood the Craft's true nature. To what did they refer? What knowledge or wisdom was being replaced by the *new* style of Freemasonry? Apparently, the long slope leading away from whatever they alluded to became even steeper as the focus on fraternalism and charities became the norm.

If Masonry is a "beautiful system of morality" and was intended to be *practiced* as a progressive art of self-transformation, then it would have taken years to advance between degrees. *How* long would depend on the commitment of the brother and the quality of instruction. But initiates (or adepts) would have spent years laboring through the lessons in each degree. In fact, we see this same method of advancement today in how Freemasonry is practiced in continental Europe, South America, and in some branches of Co-Masonry. Learning, practicing, and internalizing, the lessons that each degree offers, requires hard work and dedication.

If you are truly working the system as designed then the initiate would not advance to the next degree until he mastered the lessons of the degree he was working in. To proceed without mastering those lessons would be folly. It would make the system meaningless... a mere shell of itself. To ensure this didn't happen, the ritual itself requires the lodge officers asking the candidate over and over, in seemingly never-ending repetition if he is ready, worthy, prepared, and vouched for. We believed if the system were being utilized as designed, a candidate would only advance at the proper time. This being after he had put into practice the lessons taught in the respective degree, rather

---

[2] Wilmshurst, W.L., *The Meaning of Masonry*, 43-44.

than being rushed through so the lodge could collect his dues and issue him a card.

The leadership of the Grand Lodge of North Carolina places great emphasis on guarding the West Gate in relation to our new candidates. They want to get the right men in the front door. Men who can be transformed into the "better men" we purport to help develop. In our Grand Jurisdiction, quality is the mantra from our leadership and is considered vastly more important than quantity. But each lodge chooses who they elect to membership and, despite the Grand Lodge's emphasis on guarding the West Gate, many are so excited to have a new candidate interested in the fraternity they jump at the chance to elect and rush him through the degrees in hopes of adding new blood to their officer line. The Grand Lodge attempts to constrain this rush and confirm each candidate has achieved some level of proficiency before he is allowed to advance by maintaining a robust system of catechisms.

While ensuring a brother can repeat a catechism from memory is one way to gauge his true interest in the lessons of the degrees, it remains some distance from ensuring he has truly learned *and applied* the lessons of those degrees.

CANDIDATE ATTRITION THROUGH THE DEGREES

Over the last several years, Grand Jurisdictions across the United States have begun paying close attention to their Candidate Attrition Rates, that is, the percentage of candidates who complete each of the degrees after being elected for initiation. The graph and data below represent North Carolina's attrition rate over the last 20 years.

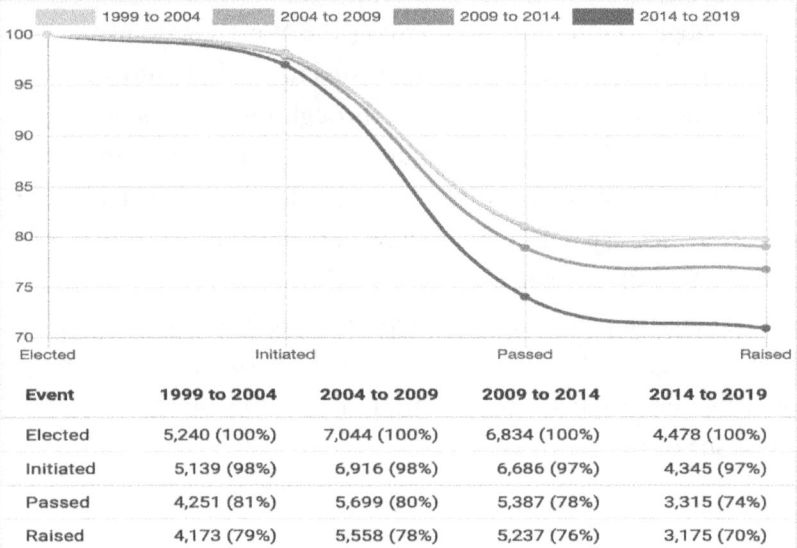

Event	1999 to 2004	2004 to 2009	2009 to 2014	2014 to 2019
Elected	5,240 (100%)	7,044 (100%)	6,834 (100%)	4,478 (100%)
Initiated	5,139 (98%)	6,916 (98%)	6,686 (97%)	4,345 (97%)
Passed	4,251 (81%)	5,699 (80%)	5,387 (78%)	3,315 (74%)
Raised	4,173 (79%)	5,558 (78%)	5,237 (76%)	3,175 (70%)

Figure 2

We can make a few interesting observations from the data. First, while the overall attrition rate has increased over the years, the general trend has remained significantly the same. Second, the data shows 17-24% of candidates quit after the Entered Apprentice degree. This is in stark contrast with the 2-3% lost before Initiation and the 2-4% who drop out between being Passed and Raised.

Something causes men to discontinue the degree work after they've been initiated. As was mentioned earlier, North Carolina requires candidates to prove proficiency in the catechism and one may assume men today don't care for the memorization. This appears to be a good explanation on the surface, however, other Grand Jurisdictions that are less strict about the proficiency requirements have higher attrition rates. We believe the attrition rate is higher after initiation because men who come to our lodges expecting an extraordinary experience, but they receive something much less transformational. They assume the Craft has an esoteric aspect to it, but the brethren they interact with after initiation are unable to satisfy their esoteric curiosity. This leaves a number of new initiates questioning if Freemasonry is what they thought it was.

Once a lodge initiates a candidate there appears to be an all-out sprint to get him to the finish, even though *in ritual* we ask him multiple times if he's worthy to proceed, yet we never evaluate his progress by any mechanism other than his proficiency with the catechism. We have no way to determine if he's applying the lessons of the degree to his life and development. To the contrary, in North Carolina our Code *requires* a candidate to proceed to the next degree within six months, otherwise he must submit a written request to continue. Eventually, he may be dropped from the rolls if he fails to progress at the corporate pace. A man can learn the words of the catechism in a few weeks yet be far from understanding the lessons of the degree he is completing. This isn't an indictment of Freemasonry, but is the situation today. "Hurry up and get them through," is the mantra. This results in the majority of brethren who joined the fraternity, including those who know all the ritualistic work, rarely taking time to consider the depth and richness of the words and symbols in our ritual. They have learned to "parrot" the words but lack understanding, sometimes not even at a surface level understanding. To many of them, the rituals are just words.

The Middle Chamber staff is keen to understand the difference between the way we believe the system was originally designed to work versus the system we currently have, while not denigrating its current state. Complaining without offering solutions is counterproductive. Bewailing that Freemasonry somehow lost its way as a Western Mystery Tradition only points out a problem that cannot be fixed. Though our numbers are in sharp decline, persuading nearly a million American Freemasons to suddenly change the system they've known their whole Masonic lives is simply not realistic.

Today's Freemasonry is a wonderful institution, made up of good and charitable men. It gives a sense of belonging and teaches foundational moral lessons. There is nothing necessarily *wrong* with Freemasonry today. Our contention, however, is that it has much more to offer than how it's commonly practiced today. While Freemasonry may currently fulfill many of our brethren's expectations, it can be much more. It holds an untapped school of arcane and universal truths. We hope to raise this aspect of the Craft from its shallow grave to claim its proper place in the Temple. This is more than teaching men how to act. It's about transforming candidates into new men, on the inside and the outside. The difference between how Freemasonry is currently practiced and what it could be to the brethren, is the difference between tracing a picture and creating art or fathering a child versus raising a child. The difference is miles apart and goes to the core of what Masonry tries to teach us.

We were convinced that Freemasonry was designed to be much more than its current state. The question was, could we create a program to teach the mysteries of the Craft effectively and could we gain permission to do so?

The permission turned out to be the easiest part. In yet another example of Providence providing the elements needed for this project, Bro. P. Shaun Bradshaw emerged as our Patron at exactly the right time. Bro. Bradshaw provided two things desperately needed if this unconventional idea was to work. Leadership and top cover. Leadership, in that he is viewed by many brethren as a natural leader and an initiate in the truest sense. Top cover, in he was the Junior Grand Warden at the time. We are blessed with wonderful, proactive, and progressive leaders in our Grand Line officers and they are always open to new ideas. But having Bro. Bradshaw as our leader helped manifest this program with minimal resistance.

The Middle Chamber instructors affectionately call Bro. Bradshaw the Patron of the program, and in every sense, he is that. Part encourager, part decision maker, part-time instructor, and full-time leader! We have no doubt that someday Masonic historians will look back on Bro. Bradshaw's legacy as well as the other brethren involved in the formation of the Middle Chamber Program, and count it as a demarcation point in the renaissance we are seeing in the Craft today.

A LITTLE RESISTANCE

When the Middle Chamber program was first discussed among some of the Grand Lodge leaders (before it even had a name) there was some disagreement on the best way to implement it. While no outright opposition existed against the program, some Grand Lodge leaders believed this type of education was 1) best suited to a lodge setting and 2) needed a way to handle the fees related to delivering the program. Some suggested it should be handled by an affinity lodge chartered just for that purpose only and the program fee would be part of the annual lodge dues. This would allow the instructors ample opportunity to teach the concepts envisioned and provide an auditable way of handling the money but it added a significant burden to the instructors and attendees in terms of administrative cost and effort. After some discussion, Bro. Bradshaw was able to convince the other Grand Lodge leaders that establishing an affinity lodge for the program was unnecessary. He developed a process instead to ensure all monies were handled appropriately and remained fully auditable.

Rather than going through a lodge to handle the money, the students signed up and paid their fees using an Eventbrite registration page or by contacting the Grand Lodge office directly. The fees collected by the Grand Lodge and are booked to the Committee on Masonic Education budget line item. Because the fees for the program materials are slightly higher than the books cost, the Middle Chamber Program became a small profit center for the Grand Lodge, and offsets the additional labor costs inherent in this program.

Chapter Four

Stones from the Quarry

In a perfect world, an initiatic school would not function on timelines. Students would simply stay in a degree until they'd learned the lessons and then advance. But the students in *this* class would be Master Masons, having already been through the degrees at the rapid rate we advance our initiates these days. So, the plan was to develop a program to take them *back* through each degree and teach them to contemplate and interpret the ritual in ways that would transform their lives. We were under no illusions we could implement a class to teach *all* the lessons a candidate should learn before being ready for the next step. This is a lifetime of work for any initiate and it will take more than a lifetime to accomplish. However, we did believe we could cover enough depth for them to understand how it was *supposed* to work and give enough of a nudge in the right direction to at least obtain the keys to their own gates. With this foundation, they could spend the balance of their days in the Craft perfecting the rushed lessons of their initiatic process, and examine them in more depth as a Middle Chamber student.

Understanding the limitations in our timelines, we decided the course work should almost a year to complete. This isn't nearly enough time to understand the depth of the lessons, but seemed a logical and practical length of time. We suspected a longer course would discourage students from participating and a shorter one would not be worth the effort. We also liked the symbology of a calendar year cycle.

The linchpin concern in building something like this was finding the right instructors. The class would succeed or fail based on instructor quality. We felt collectively that the instructor corps must have specific qualities. Every instructor didn't need all these traits, but the group had to embody them all.

First, our instructors needed a rock-solid knowledge of the ritual. In North Carolina, this means being a Class "A" certified lecturer. These brethren must know *all* the work. They are certified initially and recertified at five-year intervals by reciting the *entire* ritual from memory to a panel of peers. It is hard work and this certification typically takes years to attain. Knowing the work is not synonymous with understanding the underlying lessons that are allegorically and symbolically veiled in the words, movements, and symbols. However, one simply cannot create a program like this without a thorough knowledge of the ritualistic work. For the instructors to be credible, at least some had to be Certified Lecturers.

Next, we needed good presenters. Lecture time represents a significant portion of the course work. Proper delivery is essential. The ideas presented to students are complex and sometimes difficult to grasp. The students frequently have no basis in esoteric thought or symbol interpretation. Many have spent their lives considering their beliefs only in the way they'd been taught. Every initiatic school, including Freemasonry, invites students to reevaluate their beliefs. Instructors who could convey those demanding lessons then deal with the resulting questions clearly and concisely were essential to success.

The instructors had to be good lecturers *and* skilled with the Socratic method.

The teachers needed a background in esoteric initiatic work. This is a sensitive area to discuss but critically important. There is no doubt some Freemasons have come into a deeper level of understanding of the Craft degrees through intuition or finding a teacher within the lodge, but these are few and far between. The reality is Craft Masonry has largely lost this aspect of itself, and the brethren who understand at the deeper level learned to interpret many of those lessons from another place. Having obtained deeper knowledge and insight, they are able to view the Masonic ritual with new eyes that see its essence.

The correspondences between various Western Mystery traditions are strikingly similar, so anyone proficient in one system can easily overlay and apply those lessons to any other system. While these traditions are not exact templates of one another and differences abound, the similarities are enough where mutual understanding exists, particularly in regard to understanding the transformative nature of the ritual and symbols.

In his seminal essay, "Masonic Symbols Don't Mean: Notes on Thinking with Symbols," Dr. Jim Tresner said, "We start by learning the associations of the symbols as taught by the Masonic culture, but then, with thought, with knowledge from other sources, and by intuition, we develop them into personal symbols. They take on associations which come from our own life experiences and values. That is when they truly become powerful and valuable."

There are several keys to making this work which we will explore later, but having instructors with the proper background is critical. The nature of the course work induces robust questions from students. Instructors lacking knowledge in esoteric traditions and symbols will quickly lose credibility if they only understand the outer layer of ritual.

Fortunately, the initial group who founded this program embodied these traits and Providence[3] seemed to have been at work again. The assembled team began work on the curriculum. One of the staff members has an old tractor shed he converted into a nice work space with whiteboards and other amenities needed. Like the "hewers on the mountain, or in the quarry" the team gathered for several months to develop the program. We generated outlines with general themes divided into individual teaching blocks. These were then given to one of the instructors to develop into lesson plans for that instruction block. Every time we reconvened, we evaluated the drafted lesson plans to make suggestions and revisions. Adjustments continued as individual lessons emerged from the general outline until they were integrated into the overall plan. It was a lot of work, but... it was also a lot of fun.

We say in our ritual that by "the wisdom of Solomon...neither envy, discord, or confusion was suffered to interrupt or disturb the peace and good-fellowship which prevailed among the workmen at this important period." Similarly, we respected each other and knew we were creating something potentially groundbreaking. These were serious minded brethren who appreciated both the grandeur and sanctity of our work. Everyone was accountable and it seemed to develop smoothly. Bro. Bradshaw led the team and let the work flow with minimal input, unless we hit a problem. Then he'd encourage everyone to step back and consider the issue from different perspectives. If necessary, he provided guidance around the obstacles.

There came a day to choose a name for this new program. This may have been the most difficult decision of the whole project as the name was important. We wanted to choose wisely, but *nothing* fit. One day, near the end of the project we just started writing names on the

---

[3] While we trust that the hand of Providence guided the circumstances and people who united to create this program, we are confident it can be replicated in other jurisdictions. Our firm belief in Providence compels us to share this model with our Masonic brethren so similar programs can be spread throughout the United States.

whiteboard in every conceivable arrangement. Frustration mounted until Bro. Bradshaw uttered words from the endless combinations… "What about, The Middle Chamber Program?" Everyone stopped. The profound nature of the moment cannot be captured in words. The name eluded us throughout the process as the project rapidly came to a conclusion. This may have even been the last day we met collectively in the planning process so when the name manifested, it felt as if the cornerstone was ready to be laid in place and this phase of the work was completed.

Chapter Five

Placing the Cornerstone

The permanence and durability of the corner-stone, which lasts long after the building in whose foundation it was placed has fallen into decay, is intended to remind the Mason that, when this early house of his tabernacle shall have passed away, he has within him a sure foundation of eternal life—a corner-stone of immortality—an emanation o from that Divine Spirit which pervades all nature...

—Mackey, An Encyclopedia of Freemasonry

With the corpus of the material completed we began the implementation phase. We decided early on to begin with an introductory class in the first quarter of the year and take the next three to present the full curriculum. This fell along the lines of one class per quarter with the Entered Apprentice class in the second quarter, Fellow Craft in the third quarter, and Master Mason in the fourth quarter.

The Hook

The introductory class had multiple purposes. As with the previous Allegory and Symbolism lectures, this class occurred at four locations across the state to make it accessible to as many brethren as practical. Initially, we taught each "introductory class" on a separate weekend, methodically moving across the state. As we added more instructors, we amended this schedule to teach at all four locations on the same day, with one make up day at a single central location for brethren who missed their local class due to scheduling conflicts. We spent considerable time making the logistics work for the students, but always theorized (and eventually concluded) that the brethren truly interested in this type of instruction would travel for it, even if a bit inconvenient.

The three-hour, introductory lecture's goal is to provide an overview of the program and give students a chance to "opt in" to the remaining classes. The Middle Chamber Program deals with true initiatic work. It requires students to make a serious commitment. It is demanding of the students' time, concentration, and emotions. Most students must sacrifice other aspects of their lives to fully commit to the workload. The program's goal is to *transform* the students through understanding of the initiatic work. By design, the course is not for brethren who are simply curious or want to check the next box on their Masonic resume. The introductory course makes every possible attempt to emphasize the commitment required from the students. Freemasonry asks the initiate to express over and over the idea that his commitment is of his "own free will and accord". That phrase penetrates deeper than most understand. The student must dedicate himself to the work because he *wants* to change.

In the Middle Chamber program, we insist students take ownership of their charge. The introductory lecture dissuades curiosity seekers and bauble chasers by design. We seek only the most dedicated students. For this reason, we anticipated registration numbers would be low, perhaps only 10 or 15, since every student signed up had truly "opted in". There could be no excuses, each taking full responsibility for his own journey.

WHERE WERE YOU FIRST PREPARED?

While every Freemason knows the answer to this simple question, few have an idea of the true depth and meaning of the answer, "In my heart." A natural question that should arise is, "Prepared for what?" The short answer is, a man who wishes to join our fraternity must recognize in himself, within his heart, a need to improve who he is as a man. He must recognize he is preparing for a transformative experience. Tony Hornsby, in his book *The Rough and Rugged Road* wrote, "Initiation… is designed to give us certain experiences that allow us to discover new things about ourselves."

Only men who are prepared for transformation by our ritual, through regular contemplation of our symbols and by their association with the other members of the lodge, are prepared to receive the full value of our fraternity and thus prepared to sign a petition for membership. This is why men must come to our Craft of their "own free will and accord." Because no man, no person, can tell another when they are ready (prepared) to be transformed. That decision must be made for himself and, just like petitioning a lodge, the creators of the Middle Chamber Program believe a brother must come to this program desiring to change, to transform who he is by work, study, and contemplation.

At the end of the introductory lecture there should be no doubt in the student's mind whether he is interested or not. By the end of the day, he has either decided that he wasted three hours, or he can hardly wait to sign up. Not everyone who attends the introductory course chooses to register for the full Middle Chamber Program. Again, by design. But those who do, are *hooked*. For this reason, the staff began calling this class "The Hook." The name stuck. It retains the official name of Introductory Class but "The Hook" is the language of the instructors.

Administration

The administrative work was challenging. We had multiple issues stemming from attracting more students than anticipated. We expected to draw a dozen or so the initial year, but we had 42 sign up for the course. By the third year we had 63, then 73 in the fourth. If we'd expected to register, track, verify, collect money from, and ship books to so many students, we'd have built a more robust system from the start. This was a good problem to have, but it posed numerous challenges to work through. Yet, one idea that Brother Bradshaw pushed from his consulting background was experimentation and revision. Rather than trying to build the perfect system from the start, we should build "just enough" to get going and use feedback and experience to guide us toward better outcomes each year. The program's administration has benefited (and changed) the most from this concept.

In our first few iterations of presenting "The Hook," we mostly tracked information manually. When a student attends "The Hook," we pass around a sign-up sheet where all attendees list their name, member number, lodge, and email/phone number. This information is collected by the instructors and forwarded to the program administrator who captures it in a tracking spreadsheet. The information is also sent to the Grand Lodge office so the staff has a copy. This allows them to verify individuals signing up for the program have attended the required introductory class.

Students who are interested in signing up for the program contact the Grand Lodge, where they are guided through the registration process. We currently charge $150.00 for the program, which offsets the costs of the student packet[4]. The program materials are mailed to the students once they have paid the fee and fully registered.

---

[4] Note that the instructor corps providing this service on behalf of the Grand Lodge of North Carolina have, as of this book's writing, provided their time and travel on a pro-bono basis. We could charge more for the program to offset some instructor costs, but we intend to make this program financially accessible to our brethren.

True to our experimentation approach, as of 2020, we began using Eventbrite for student registration. This helps with collecting program fees and ensures the program administrator and Grand Lodge office staff stay in sync with who has signed up for the program.

The mailed student packets include five textbooks and a journal. The Grand Lodge Office procures 40-50 copies of each book prior to the start of the program, which minimizes delays sending the packets to the students. It also reduces the likelihood the vendors won't have the books when needed. Once the packet is mailed, the program administrator emails students the initial reading assignments, which they are expected to have read prior to the Entered Apprentice class. We learned the hard way in our first year to set a hard cutoff date for all registrations, otherwise the Grand Lodge office will not have time to distribute the packets and track which students are officially registered for the class. The cutoff date marks the point where students are transferred from the Grand Lodge office to our "in house" Middle Chamber program administrator who handles all further correspondence.

There are two more important points on having the registration process go through the Grand Lodge office. First, we want to be careful in who handles the money. This process simplifies collecting student fees by removing the middleman and ensuring all monies go directly to the Grand Lodge. Second, it helps solidify the students' perception that the program is legitimate and sanctioned by the Grand Lodge. A major factor in this program's success is it's an official, Grand Lodge sanctioned educational course. This gives it a greater level of credibility and allays potential concerns from the students that it could be spurious in some way. Having the registration process handled by the Grand Lodge administrative staff reiterates this intent.

Student Packets

The student kits contain the following five books, which are ordered, stocked, and shipped by the Grand Lodge. They are:

1. *The Meaning of Masonry* by Walter Leslie Wilmshurst

2. *Freemasonry, It's Hidden Meaning* by George Steinmetz

3. *The Way of the Craftsman* by Kirk MacNulty

4. *Contemplative Masonry* by Chuck Dunning

5. *The Initiatic Experience* by Robert Herd

The students also receive a nice leather-bound journal to record their personal reflections.

Freemasonry has many legitimate and important facets. We are Fraternal. We are Charitable. We are Civic Minded. We have a rich history of members' impacts on national and world events. These aspects of the Fraternity are worthy endeavors and the Middle Chamber does not aim to dissuade or disparage any of them. This program is designed to be the cornerstone for introducing members to the *spiritual* and *philosophical* aspects of our ritual.

All the authors whose books we chose approach Freemasonry from this same aspect. They are part of a larger group of like-minded Masonic thinkers who include the likes of Albert Mackey, Albert Pike, George Oliver, and numerous others. Again, we are careful to point out we are not trying to change every aspect of Freemasonry or dissuade our brethren in any way from the fraternal and charitable parts of our fraternity. That's neither possible nor practical. We are, however, attempting to give spiritual water to a long-neglected flower in the garden of the Craft. Afterall, there are three principal tenets of a Mason's profession: Brotherly Love, Relief, and **Truth**. This program focuses on the third tenet: Truth - and attempts to bring it into equal footing with the other two more prominent tenets.

Chapter Six

The Porch

In the ancient initiations, the candidate was never permitted on the threshold of the temple or sacred cavern, in which the ceremonies were conducted, until by the most solemn warning he had been impressed with the necessity of caution, secrecy, and fortitude.

—Bahnson, North Carolina Lodge Manual

The Middle Chamber courses are continually refined, but the basic premise has remained the same. The initiate's development through the degrees focuses on three major elements of his life: the physical, the psychical, and the spiritual, with each degree corresponding to one element. The Holy Royal Arch degree is beyond the Middle Chamber Program's scope, but it's acknowledged here for the critical place it holds as the Capstone of the Craft degree system and corresponds to the divine element of life.

The authors of the books listed in the previous chapter align philosophically in their interpretation of ritual and symbols, though they approach them from different angles. Wilmshurst and Steinmetz are mystics. MacNulty is a Kabbalist. Chuck Dunning is a Contemplative and Rob Herd is a pragmatist using a comparative Western Mystery Tradition concept. Although each uses a different approach, they can be grouped together as Masonic philosophers who view the Work in the same way... there are many *truths* concealed within our ritual. We chose each book carefully and for multiple reasons. We believe these texts give students a diverse perspective of Masonic philosophy while aligning on their view of Masonic ritual embodying universal truths. Cost, availability, and keeping the reading list at a manageable level necessitated leaving some exceptional books out. But we encouraged students to build their own Masonic library (see Appendix A for a detailed list of suggested books).

Although each author uses terminology associated with his own personal approach, the program establishes some fundamental truths that span them all. This work does not teach the whole program, but these key principles are explained.

The first *truth* the students must learn is, our ritual is "veiled in allegory and illustrated by symbols." We say these words to every initiate, but the lesson is often missed. Not *every* teaching of Masonry is dependent on understanding the power of this phrase, but the Work of the Middle Chamber student is fundamentally tied to it. For him, it's as if there's a divergence in the path when hearing this phrase. He recognizes he now stands before the pillars Boaz and Jachin, "in the porch of King Solomon's Temple." In this porch, which is emblematic of life's transitory nature, he must decide to enter the Temple and explore the depths of allegory and symbols, or remain outside, satisfied with the surface-level explanations of the ritual.

Our degrees mirror changes that occur throughout a man's life and sometimes inspire those changes. As a result, the Middle Chamber program was intentionally designed so the student continuously finds himself back "in the porch." Our hope is, each time he passes through it, he gains a greater understanding of the Craft, its symbols, and himself.

The casual member may stay on the threshold and walk the wide and well-worn path of conventional Freemasonry. But the "veiled in allegory and illustrated by symbols" reference introduces the *Masonic Initiate* to an alternate Path of interpreting and understanding the ritual. This is the Narrow Path that lies past the threshold and leads an Initiate to the *esoteric* world of allegories and symbolism.

44

The Initiate understands the exoteric teachings of the degrees in the same manner as every fraternal member. Good, noble lessons that all men should strive to achieve. The virtues, the tenets, the inspirations, ethics and morals, science and reason... just to name a few, are presented as we progress through the degrees. They empower a man to contemplate his life and apply the lessons of Freemasonry to improve himself. We are taught in the Entered Apprentice Degree Charge that the practice of these virtues will lead him to "public and private esteem."

However, to the Initiate who searches deeper, there's a more transformative Path. Let's be honest, most fraternal members don't take a holistic approach to personal change by employing the ideas presented in the degrees. We metaphorically walk through the orchard of ritual occasionally picking an appealing life lesson and putting it into practice. Yet, how many seek to become the gardener? Who amongst us seeks to nurture the entire crop so we may someday partake of the entire bounty? The answer is, extremely few of us. But we present this approach to the Middle Chamber student. When properly practiced, the ritual provides a map to our personal hero's journey.

In the Kingdom of Saudi Arabia

— Bro. Ben's Own Hero's Journey —

In 1991 I found myself stationed at Dhahran Air Base in Saudi Arabia. I was a young USAF Staff Sergeant Crash/Fire/Rescue specialist. When we arrived, we learned we'd be housed in the Saudi fire station as the Saudis had consolidated into one side of the firehouse, giving the Americans the vacated side. This placed us in close proximity with our Saudi (and all Muslim) counterparts. We'd spend months together training and executing our mission.

I grew up in the Southern Baptist Church in rural North Carolina. During my formative years, I was assured anyone who wasn't a Christian was doomed to the eternal fiery pit of Hell. Although my religious practices declined during my adult years, I still held this belief firmly. I wasn't keen on the idea of being in such close contact with my infidel colleagues. I wasn't a zealous Christian, but I didn't want their heathen ways to rub off on me. This attitude, a result of my upbringing and ignorance, was all I knew of religion as a young man of twenty-four.

However, several things happened during my time with the Saudis that set me on my own Hero's Journey and changed me at a fundamental level. I went from my old "normal" to a completely "new normal" in how I viewed my religious beliefs and those of others. Indeed, the journey began when I was deployed literally halfway around the world, from Eielson AFB in Alaska to the Kingdom of Saudi Arabia.

Being immersed in a culture of a different faith challenged me. I thought it abominable. However, Providence provided a guide although I didn't realize it at the time. His name was Alex, a Senior Airman from the Philadelphia area. A bright, articulate, professional young man assigned to my shift, we hadn't met prior to this deployment, but we developed a mutual respect for each other. One day Alex and I were talking and he casually mentioned he had visited with local Imams set up outside the Air Base. They were actively recruiting potential converts. Alex revealed his family was Muslim and while he had fallen from his faith, his experience in Saudi Arabia seemed to be drawing him back. Astonished to hear this from my friend, including his background, I couldn't fathom him returning to Islam. Alex was a firefighter like us. He was American, a normal guy. How could he possibly be one of "them"? The discussion shook me to my core and forced me on a path of examining my own beliefs. In one casual conversation, my guide rocked my belief system, unknowingly setting me on a journey to enlightenment.

I not only observed Alex over the following months, I came to know the Saudi firefighters as well. And… they were good guys. While there were cultural differences, they were normal firefighters like the Americans. They had many of the same issues we did. When they finished work, they took their kids to the dentist and to soccer practice. They helped with homework and managed family affairs. We worked and trained together, doing the same job in the same professional manner. Slowly, my opinions changed. Through ongoing discussions with Alex about Islam and my budding friendship with the Saudis, I began to question my beliefs. One minute I would fall back on my religious dogma that claimed these brothers were doomed to Hell because they were not Christians. The next, I saw them as normal guys, living their lives much as I did back home. Except, they'd grown up in a different religion. It made me wonder what my beliefs would be had I been born into their culture?

These thoughts culminated one cloudy day under contemplation so deep, I had an epiphany. Suddenly, I was overcome with the realization that I did not believe these brother firefighters were going to Hell. In an instant, my belief system changed. As the realization washed over me, I felt freed from something haunting me for some time. I'd broken free from a perceived truth; one I then knew was false. In that moment, my world changed.

In my irrational 24-year-old mind, I surmised that if this particular aspect of my religious teaching was not true, then all those teachings must be false. I found myself with a new normal in my thinking. Prior to deployment, I held a firm belief about my religion. A journey to an alien land led me to a guide. By challenging my dogma, this guide propelled me on a path where I'd battle my beliefs. The Saudi firefighters were all players on this journey as every one of their stories became a new battle within my mind. In the end, I won a victory over a dogmatic belief and returned to the United States with a new normal in my religious understanding and tolerance.

However, this Hero's Journey was simply the beginning of several journeys that played out over several decades. The new normal I gained coming out of the Kingdom of Saudi Arabia suggested my religious system was wrong and broken. I spurned religion entirely for many years. Freemasonry brought me back to it to examine my spirituality. That became another Hero's Journey that would end in my return to Christianity, albeit by seeing with new eyes and hearing with new ears. But that story is for a different day.

While personal perfection eludes each of us, the Middle Chamber program presents the lessons of our ritual as a Path to wholeness. But the initiate can't simply cherry pick his way to enlightenment. He must be wholly committed to applying Freemasonry's lessons to his life. If he does this, through years of study, labor, and an unrelenting commitment, he can discover a New Man within. By applying the knowledge gained he can become not only a better version of himself but from his old *self* emerges a new *Self*. Not only improved but transformed. In a sense, his old essence must die to be regenerated in a new form. MacNulty describes it this way: "It is the Self, symbolized by the Junior Warden in the lodge and the Junior Grand Warden in the traditional history, that 'dies'. That Self is the individual, the resident of the Psychological World, who must be true to his principles and surrender his will (which he has worked so hard to attain)."[5]

However, in order to travel this "dark and difficult path" he first must understand the *truth* of *veiled* and *illustrated*. He must realize the lessons presented to all Masons embody secondary meanings for those who seek them. Helping the students discover these esoteric, or hidden, ritualistic lessons, is the work of the Middle Chamber staff, while staying within Masonic teachings as expounded by Masonic philosophers and the textbook authors.

---

[5] MacNulty, W. Kirk, *The Way of the Craftsman*, 137.

48

Given the necessity to understand the nature of Masonic allegories, two ideas are communicated early and often. The first is the allegory of our buildings and the second is the mind as a model of our psyche.

The degrees use two edifices as metaphors to convey much of the work: The Lodge and the Temple. The first structure our ritual is built around is the Lodge. Over and over in our ritual, actions take place *in*, and explanations are given *of*, the Lodge. As the degrees progress, the Lodge slowly yields to the grander idea of the Temple, similar to the initiate giving in to a grander manifestation of himself. The use of these two grand buildings teaches many lessons. But one shining Truth that all initiates should know is, both the Lodge and the Temple are *you*! Allegorically, you are the Lodge. You are the Temple. With this is realization, the meanings behind the initiatic teachings are seen through new eyes. Every explanation, every storyline, every officer, every piece of furniture, every working tool, every action, and every symbol in the Lodge or Temple are illuminating some aspect of the initiate about himself. In the ritual we discuss the architecture and contents of the physical building, but that is the *exoteric* explanation. It also has a *veiled* allusion. The Lodge and Temple are metaphors for the consciousness of the initiate. Further, progress from the concept of the Building, to the Lodge, to the Temple, symbolically represents the physical, psychical and spiritual nature of the individual, respectively.

THE LODGE IS YOU: AN ESOTERIC EXPLANATION

Bro. Bradshaw led a program for a lodge on the esoteric nature of our ritual. Near the beginning, he asked the brethren what they thought the Lodge represented. The consensus was, the Tabernacle or King Solomon's Temple. Bro. Bradshaw confirmed our ritual says the Lodge represents these structures, but it begs the question: What do those structures represent? He pointed out, our ritual frequently provides explanations, which are intended to further our thinking about the symbols. He asked, "What does King Solomon's Temple represent to you?" Many of the brethren weren't sure, because they'd never learned to contemplate any meaning beyond the ritual's given explanation. But a couple of brethren observed that King Solomon's Temple was a physical structure in which the divine presence, the *shekinah*, dwelled. Similar to King Solomon's Temple, our bodies are a physical structure in which the divine spark of Deity, our soul, dwells.

After a few minutes of contemplation, they understood why we say, "The Lodge is *you*."

Another fundamental truth is the meaning behind the three principal officers. All authors we use for the program subscribe to an idea that the three principal officers represent specific aspects of your consciousness. Additionally, MacNulty assigns all officers of the lodge a place in his allegorical interpretation of the lodge as a model for the psyche. In his book *The Way of the Craftsman*, he explains the Worshipful Master represents the Spiritual aspect of consciousness, the Senior Warden the Psychological or Soul, and the Junior Warden the Self. The Senior Deacon represents an awakening as he *guides* the candidate through the ritual. The Junior Deacon functions as feeling or intuition and, in American workings where we do not use an Inner Guard, also serves as the Ego. The Tyler represents the psyche's connection to the physical body. The other chosen authors use slightly different wording and interpretations, but all ascribe to the same concept, the lodge and everything associated with it allegorically is a symbol of the Initiate.

These fundamental truths are intrinsically accepted by members who view Freemasonry as a Western Mystery system. Again, these are the first concepts we present to the Middle Chamber students and it's absolutely critical they understand these principles to begin their journey toward building and adorning their own Temples.

It's often said that Masonry is a progressive art. You simply cannot advance to more complex concepts until you've learned and applied the fundamental ideas that serve as a foundation. The coursework trains the students to take this approach as they reflect upon the ritual and symbols. Conveyed another way, candidates are *initially* hastened through the degrees in the same manner all American Masons experienced. In the Middle Chamber Program, the students' journey through the degrees and are re-exposed to the lessons. Slowly and methodically, the instructors reveal great hidden meanings of the degrees. But knowing a year is not enough time for the development required, students are expected to return and continue the hard work of an initiate. Indeed, "Masonry is work."

The initial exposure to the Middle Chamber course teaches students the curriculum. But to ensure their success as students of the Work, they must commit to continuing their education through subsequent exposures to the program. This is where real change occurs. Receiving the degrees in the lodge gives them the foundation. The Middle Chamber Program gives them the knowledge - the keys to interpretation. But the path to transformation lies in a lifetime of interior work true initiates perform for themselves.

Our hope is, by their own free will and accord, students will painstakingly master the foundational lessons and become a living embodiment of the virtues. Then, they can harness the ego to discover their relationship with the universe and Deity. Thousands of lessons, large and small, are learned and applied until finally, they are presented with the ultimate heartbreaking and exhilarating lesson that is both the beginning and the end. Having become true Master Masons in the *initiatic* sense, by applying the lessons of the degrees they labored so hard to attain, they now must lay their hard-won victory on the altar of sacrifice and, of their own free will and accord, yield control to the Great Architect of the Universe.

Chapter Seven

Middle Chamber

[This] pictorial representation of an ascent by a winding staircase to the place where the wages of labor were to be received, was an allegory to teach us the ascent of the mind from ignorance, through all the toils of study and the difficulties of obtaining knowledge, receiving here a little and there a little, adding something to the stock of our ideas at each step, until, in the middle chamber of life—in the full fruition of manhood—the reward is attained, and the purified and elevated intellect is invested with the reward in the direction how to seek God and God's truth...

—Mackey, An Encyclopedia of Freemasonry

As the students begin the course work, they transition from the excitement and glamour of being part of a new journey into the grind of actually doing the Work.

After attending the Introductory Class, registering for the program, and receiving their student packet, they receive their first instructions from the Middle Chamber staff. These include initial reading assignments and homework in preparation for the Entered Apprentice class generally held in the second quarter of the year.

Assignments are given between classes as the year progresses and by the end of it the students should have read all the books and completed all assignments. Human nature means some will not complete all the homework or reading assignments. Like all classrooms, students run the full spectrum of human learning modalities. There are auditory learners, visual learners, and kinesthetic learners. There are different personality types and complex varieties of experiences and backgrounds. The instructors understand this and try to provide information in multiple forms to best deliver the lessons to every student. Using a mix of lecture, videos, reading, interactive exercises, one-on-one discussion, and Q&A, the instructors hope to reach every class member in a meaningful way.

But one prevailing belief among the instructors is that this material cannot be presented in a purely academic environment. When discussing this class to other Masonic educators across the country, we are frequently asked for our PowerPoint presentations. We have purposefully refrained from developing this method of delivery. Although the lectures follow a basic outline and fairly strict schedule, the instructors are open to the organic nature of instruction. To some extent, this allows the students to help drive where the instruction needs to go.

While we do have a set of outlines and associated timelines we use for continuity, the body of the lectures come from the staff's knowledge. The instructors teach the lessons in their own styles, interjecting their own experiences and understandings. This is only possible when teachers have a firm grasp of the material presented, the lessons imparted, and an excellent rapport with each other. As long as the main talking points are covered and the lessons remain grounded in Masonry, the instructors are free to deliver the instruction in their own individual styles. Because we attempt to blend highly personal *initiatic* work with *academic* work in a classroom setting, we find this method works best by striking a delicate balance between intimate discussions at the core of one's being, while adhering to the syllabus and schedule. The transfer of information to the students is a vitally important aspect of this course, but the awakening of understanding usually occurs when talking *with* them... not *at* them. That's really our true mission... to help them sense when and how a symbol or part of the ritual resonates with them rather than teach them another set of dogmatic interpretations learned by rote. We strive to present a framework for interpreting the ritual and symbols in ways that speak to them and affect real, transformative change.

That said, we've developed a robust, but not regimented, set of lesson plans with talking points we share with new instructors. While our delivery is eclectic, these core lesson plans, which include major themes and takeaways for each section, keep us on track and on time.

The author's and philosopher's textbooks provided, as well as the additional recommended reading list in Appendix A, exemplify the interpretations used to teach the class. Those books are easily purchased and any interested Mason should possess copies in his personal library. They form the corpus of the coursework and the lessons taught in the Middle Chamber Program draw directly from them. These texts subscribe to the idea that the Entered Apprentice degree embodies lessons of our physical existence, the Fellow Craft of our psychological aspect, and the Master Mason of our spiritual essence and aligns with the Kabbalistic concept of the Four Worlds. The erudite Mason will find much wisdom in the recommended books. Due to the size and scope of these resources, we'll give the briefest of summaries on the major themes taught in the program.

THE FOUR WORLDS

In his book, *The Way of the Craftsman*, Bro. W. Kirk MacNulty draws parallels between the Kabbalistic concept of the **Four Worlds** and the explanation given in the Masonic lectures on the importance of Geometry, the fifth science and "the one most esteemed by Masons."

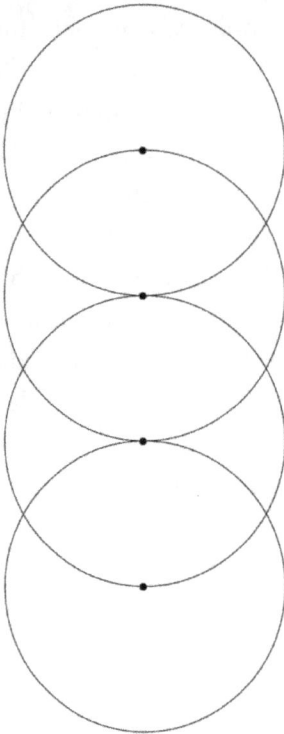

Dimensions of
Consciousness

World of Divinity
(Divine Consciousness)

World of Spirit
(Sanctum Sanctorum)
Free Will – Attitude toward fate in
fulfilling destiny

World of Psyche
(Middle Chamber)
Destiny – Purpose; reason for
existence

World of Physicality
(Outside the Temple)
Fate – What Providence provides
(tools)

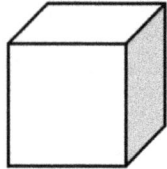

Figure 3

At the bottom is the World of Physicality and can be compared to a cube, or a solid, which "is a figure of three dimensions, namely, length, breadth, and thickness." This represents conscious, creative thought and intellect. Through this aspect of our consciousness we perceive, interpret, and interact with our physical reality.

Next is the World of Psyche. This World is likened to the superficies, which "is a figure of two dimensions, namely, length and breadth" and symbolizes our emotional and intuitive sense. This part of our selves is built upon personal experiences and may cause us to act (or react) in ways we do not consciously comprehend.

Third in the line is the World of Spirit, which corresponds to the line, "a figure of one capacity, namely, length." Those who spend time in consistent contemplative practice may, on occasion, glimpse the profound influence this level of consciousness wields over our behavior.

At the top is the World of Divinity. It corresponds to a point, which "is a dimensionless figure, or an indivisible part of space." Like the point, Divine Consciousness is also "dimensionless" and therefore limitless in the possibilities of creation. As the point is the singularity from which the line is derived, and from the line to the superficies, and from the superficies to the solid, so too is the Divine Consciousness the singularity from which our own consciousness is derived.

Entered Apprentice

The Entered Apprentice degree teaches lessons about our existence in this physical world and our interactions with everything in it, especially each other.

In the ritual, we ask the candidate multiple times, "Who comes here?" The members of a lodge certainly know the man's name, his occupation, his family status, and much more. The question is posed to the initiate for *his* contemplation. He is being asked who he *really* is. Not at a superficial level, but beyond that. "Who comes here?" is a prevailing theme throughout the initiatic experience and is introduced at the beginning of our Masonic journey.

To teach brethren who they are, it's necessary to first teach them who they are not. The Entered Apprentice degree requires an exploration of the *Self* versus the *self* or the True Self against the false self. Everyone plays different roles in life. Father, teacher, husband, employee, boss, coach, counselor, and so on. As well-rounded humans, we *must* play these roles. A man who always plays only one role will be ineffective at times. Try wearing your "boss persona" while talking to your wife or your "lover persona" while chatting with a coworker. Each will result in bad outcomes. The lesson is not about removing all masks, but understanding their true nature so they don't rule you. The student learns to differentiate between these universal masks we wear "in our several stations before God and man." They are encouraged to discover their True Self, beyond the "masks" of their false self. "Who comes here?" is a more complex and difficult question than most brethren contemplate.

The concept of materialism is introduced in the preparation room and continues throughout the degree to the last working tool. How can we advance to study and understand the great lessons of the Fellow Craft and Master Mason degrees if we obsess over and are controlled by our material world *stuff*? Clearly, some *stuff* is necessary, like jobs and homes, insurance and electricity. Other *stuff* is unnecessary, like golf and fishing, football and beer. No one is suggesting we become Masonic monks and give up the fun stuff in life. Conversely, we all know men so caught up in the torrent of life they don't work on becoming better people. You don't have to give up the worldly life, but don't let it rule you.

Finally, the degree offers how we should conduct ourselves in this life… the ideals fundamental to our advancement.

The Principal Tenets of Brotherly Love, Relief, and Truth provide an opportunity to explore who a Man is at his essence. Do we need to be *taught* how to love our neighbors as ourselves, to be charitable to our fellow beings, and to pursue Truth? Or are these innate qualities born within us? Have we fallen away from these ideals? How should we return? Are we *truly* trying to embody or practice the Tenets? Or do we simply pay them lip service?

The Theological and Cardinal Virtues have been stepping-stones in the Temples of Initiates for aeons. In his book *Living Theurgy*, Kupperman quotes the great Western Mystery teacher, Plotinus, as saying "…when the Soul…(is) at first disengaged from the body, it concentrates on itself; then it abandons its own habits, withdrawing from discursive into intellect's thought; finally, at its third stage, it is possessed by the divine and drifts into an extraordinary serenity befitting the gods rather than men."[6]

Kupperman explains, "Plotinus sees the Virtues allowing us to rise above our entrapment in the world of matter, bringing us closer to the gods and God. Engagement with the virtues on this level bring about the purification of the Soul so that it may fully remember itself as being a divine being and, ultimately, rise above and withdraw from physical manifestation, if only temporarily. For Plotinus, the purified soul does not need to remain at this high level, and, while still incarnate, may descend to employ the civic virtues in a perfected way. For Iamblicus, this descent is a necessity of the dual-natured human Soul."[7]

---

[6] Kupperman, Jeffery, *Living Theurgy*, 52.

[7] Kupperman, Jeffery, *Living Theurgy*, 52.

The Entered Apprentice degree reminds us to *practice* the virtues to become better versions of ourselves, but the true initiate hopes someday to *become* the living embodiment of the virtues. In his essay "On Friendship", Cicero states, "Virtute enim ipsa no tam mulit praediti esse quam videri volunt." [Few are those who wish to be endowed with virtue rather than to seem so.]

For too many fraternal members, there appears to be a satisfaction simply to *seem* virtuous, to *act* in a virtuous manner, but neglect the real change that must occur internally. They act the part, do charitable work, attend meetings (sometimes), but do not internalize the lessons of the Virtues within themselves. The Middle Chamber Program works to clear up that distinction and encourages the brethren to improve their thoughts, words and deeds.

BECOMING THE VIRTUES

One of the Middle Chamber instructors, Bro. Randy Browning, relates an experience at the Masonic Restoration Foundation Symposium in Philadelphia in 2015. He and a group of Masons headed to dinner following the days' events, everyone dressed in their finest attire and feeling smug in their Masonic circle of influence. Upon leaving the restaurant, the group walked back to the hotel with the sidewalk width forcing them to walk two abreast, forming a long line.

The downtown section of Philadelphia has an evident homeless population and from the tail end of the line, Randy watched the brethren as they walked past homeless people asking for alms. Randy had a sudden epiphany. Freemasonry teaches us about the Tenets and the Virtues, but there he was turning a blind eye to an opportunity to practice them. Worse was the paradoxical feeling of attending a conference to learn the "best practices" in Masonry, while ignoring a fundamental Tenet of the Craft. The moment was profound.

In that instant, he looked down to a young homeless woman. His eyes locked with hers and he saw not only a destitute soul, but his own soul reflected in return. He reached into his pocket and gave her all the cash he had. But more than money, by the Tenet of Relief, he gave her hope. It shone in her eyes. The mutual recognition of one soul truly seeing another in all of its vulnerability. This opportunity provided a lesson of not only *learning* the Tenets, but *practicing* them, and ultimately *becoming* them.

To this day, Randy wonders which soul the Grand Architect intended this lesson to affect more.

Fellow Craft

Progressing from the degree of the material world toward the final destination of the spiritual world, we must transition through the "mind-stuff" as Wilmshurst calls it.

Advancing from the lessons of the Entered Apprentice degree, with one foot remaining in the world of materialism, we move increasingly deeper within ourselves. Focusing predominantly on the lecture of the second-degree, we introduce the concepts of dualities and trinities.

The pillars, Jachin and Boaz, present a striking example of Kabbalistic instruction. How can two seemingly opposing concepts be married to create a new concept? How can the introduction of a third concept create yet another? Can a thing be more than the sum of its parts? Do the pillars represent a duality, a trinity, or both? Or are they simply the constituent parts of a thing?

How can the Orders of Architecture represent the ideas of God's creation and how does it relate to us? Did the Divine Creator have a blueprint on his celestial trestle board? Does sacred geometry bind the order of nature, humankind, and the Orders of Architecture together? How are our limited senses calculated into the equation?

Mastering the Seven Liberal Arts and Sciences makes us learned men, but *why* is it important? Can only intelligent men master the lesson of the third degree? To what end do we use the information gained from the study of these arts? Or is the lesson simply that certain subjects must be understood for one to advance and, if so, do the Seven Liberal Arts and Sciences actually symbolize subjects other than the trivium and quadrivium?

THE GOLDEN RATIO

The Golden Ratio, sometimes referred to as the Divine Proportion, is observed throughout nature and was used extensively in Greek architecture. In mathematics, this irrational number is represented by the Greek letter phi:[8]

$$\varphi = \frac{1 + \sqrt{5}}{2} = 1.6180339887\ldots.$$

This Divine Proportion is also found in the proportion of the various segments of the pentagram or Blazing Star, found in the center of the mosaic pavement of the Lodge and hieroglyphically represents Divine Providence, which all Masons are taught to rely upon faithfully.

[9]

The preceding lessons lay important groundwork for the transition that follows. The initiate who understands and controls the difference

---

[8] Weisstein, Eric W. "Golden Ratio". mathworld.wolfram.com.Retrieved 2020-08-10

[9] https://en.m.wikipedia.org/wiki/Golden_ratio#/media/File%3A Pentagram-phi.svg

between the false self and True Self, who acts through his will rather than reacts through an animalistic and base nature, has passed through the pillars of Jachin and Boaz. The initiate who has mastered his obsession with worldly possessions, lives the Tenets, embodies the Virtues, and understands how his constituent parts make a complex whole, has climbed the winding staircase. The initiate who sees himself for what he is in creation, understands his limitations, and has obtained and applies the knowledge available to him, is ready to cross the river of sacrifice to a yet deeper place within himself. The initiate, coming so far of his own free will and accord, is presented again with the idea of sacrifice. The corn, the river, Jeptha (judge of Israel), remind us allegorically that to become a new version of ourselves, we must die to our old selves. Both cannot exist at the same time.

Having separated our True Self from our old outward *self*, we are ready to pass our final inner guardian to gain entrance to *our* Middle Chamber. This is a place deep within our own psyche, is near the center of our being and at the entrance of our Sanctum Sanctorum. There we find the altar and the wages of our sacrifice.

> *Here, then, is the true wage of the Fellow-Craft: the corn which nourishes his physical body, provided by the all-wise beneficence of his creator, truly a "gift from God"; oil, the refresher of his physical body, that which "makes his face to shine." More mystically interpreted, the ointment which sets him apart from others, which makes him the "appointed" of God. And finally, wine, which as Grant says, is "not the wine of men, but the ecstatic inflow of a religious mystic experience"-the summation of his labors, the award for the arduous ascent of the three, five and seven steps of the winding stairs."*
>
> *- Steinmetz*[10]

---

[10] Steinmetz, George H., *Freemasonry: Its Hidden Meaning*, 134.

MIDDLE CHAMBER

Master Mason

For time's sake, the course work briefly touches on the ritual and symbols of the first section, but focuses mainly on the second section of the Master Mason degree. Here the initiate takes the mantle of the Master Hiram, enters *his own* Inner Chamber, draws his designs upon *his own* trestle board and begins *his own* hero's journey toward personal enlightenment.

The degree features an unfinished temple. A missing Grand Master. A lost Word. Absent craftsmen. All symbols of incompletion. The man who believes he's complete and perfect is a fool. As men are we not all, to varying degrees, incomplete and imperfect? To strive for that perfection is the noble cause of man and Mason. Isn't it incumbent upon him to strive for the lofty goal of perfection and, although never reached, at least become a better version of himself in the process? The best among us who rests on his laurels and proclaims himself good enough has missed the entire point of being human.

In our journeys, don't we all encounter our own ruffians? As Masons we receive this example to force us to consider *our* true nature. The ruffians are wayward workmen from *our* Temple. They have slain *our* Master. They have tried and failed to escape *our* country. And for a time, they have disrupted the work of *our* Craftsmen and laid us in the rubbish of *our* Temple.

We *are* the Temple. We *are* the Lodge.

These elements of ritual are also elements of us. The Middle Chamber Program strives to ensure students understand this.

Eventually initiates will assemble their best attributes and highest qualities. They can then purge themselves of their lower, more base properties. These are our Craftsmen and our Ruffians. Once the obstacles are removed, the true Master Mason reunites the *dual* aspects of his Spiritual and Psychological nature to fill his empty chair and create a *triune* and harmonious version of himself symbolized by the equilateral triangle and formed by the placement of the three principal officers in the lodge.

Chapter Eight

Inner Chamber

But thou, when thou prayest, enter into thine inner chamber, and having shut thy door, pray to thy Father who is in secret, and thy Father who seeth in secret shall recompense thee.

—Matthew 6:6 (American Standard Version)

From the beginning of the Middle Chamber Program, we wanted to offer the students an advanced class beyond the existing curriculum. While the program had a natural ending point, more work remained. The curriculum provided the students with a deeper understanding of the ritual, as well as an appreciation that further "Masonic labor" was necessary, but questions arose about how the students should do that work. The program's core lessons established a foundation for something more profound.

In the Middle Chamber Program, students learn from lecture, interaction, reading assignments, and various types of homework. This creates an effective learning environment, but it mainly focuses on presenting material that allows for self-reflection by the students. The in-person interactions effectively conveyed the ideas we focused on, but the scope of those ideas was limited.

We believed we could create an experience that enhanced the group work aspect by putting into practice several concepts we'd discussed in the classroom. Specifically, we wanted to explore the idea of the Lodge as a model of the psyche, as advanced by the authors of our textbooks. If the lodge is supposed to represent you, and you are supposed to labor in and on your own Temple, then the lesson is to actively labor within your own existence, or "Interior work," as Kirk MacNulty calls it. In the assignments and discussions, we examine this concept throughout the year. We explain it in multiple ways, design brief group activities around it, remind students their textbooks focus on it, and attempt to advance it in every aspect of the curriculum. But time constraints prevent us from delving too deeply into individual and group activities where the students can practice the ideas we've spent a year teaching them. Some students find a way to practically apply these concepts on their own, perhaps having already practiced interior work before starting the program. Others have difficulty making the leap from *learning* the concept to *applying* it, but we sensed many students were on the threshold and needed a final push into the world of *applying the lessons* for personal transformation.

Like the Middle Chamber Program, it took a few years to develop the Inner Chamber. The first two years we focused on creating and refining the Middle Chamber's initial curriculum, but by the third year, we'd settled into a zone that allowed devoted time and energy toward creating the advanced course.

We examined many options, but settled on a weekend retreat model. The Freemasons of North Carolina are one of the few remaining Grand Jurisdictions who still own and operate a campus for our children's home. The Masonic Home for Children at Oxford (MHCO) is located in Oxford, NC, about an hour north of Raleigh. Its first incarnation in 1858 started as St. John's College, but was repurposed as an orphanage in 1873. It remains open today and serves over 50 children ranging from infants to college-aged, independent-living students. The beautiful campus has a palpable energy fostered by nearly 150 years of love and support heaped on the children we Freemasons are obligated to relieve. Today the children mostly reside in a cul-de-sac of newer buildings away from the main entrance, but many old red brick dormitories remain and contribute to an ageless feeling pervading the campus. For multiple reasons, the "Children's Home," as it is known in North Carolina, was a *good* logistical choice for the retreat. The feeling one gets standing on its grounds makes it the *perfect* choice.

As mentioned, one of the textbooks used in the course is *Contemplative Masonry* by Bro. Chuck Dunning. This book delves deeply into the practical aspect of applying lessons of the ritual in your own psyche. One particular exercise presents the idea of a mental lodge, which is imprinted in every Freemason's mind, as an internal retreat when seeking answers to life's questions. Bro. Dunning is a frequent speaker on the national Masonic circuit and the decision to invite him to help facilitate the retreat was an easy one.

To ensure attendees understood their coming journey, as well as the program's seriousness, alumni underwent a rigorous application process. Seventeen dedicated Middle Chamber Program graduates attended the newly dubbed Inner Chamber retreat.

We built the curriculum around a single, profound exercise. The MHCO campus boasts an intimate lodge room in one of the old dormitories, which we converted into a live version of the *mental* lodge used in the exercise Bro. Dunning describes in his book. The remainder of the retreat's lectures and activities were developed to ensure students were fully prepared for the experience.

Students arrived on Friday evening and after registering and eating, immediately commenced work. We began by introducing the Holy Royal Arch degree as a completion of the Craft degrees. Although both the Middle and Inner Chamber work focuses on Craft Masonry, we believed it appropriate to provide the historical context and philosophical importance of this degree. We then set the tone for the next day by challenging students to form a question or idea they'd bring into the lodge the next day. They needed to prepare to address their inquiry to the stations and places in the lodge when the main exercise commenced. They were told this was serious work and the questions to ask themselves should be profound. The students rose to the challenge.

The following day, another classroom workshop further prepared the students by mentally walking them through what they'd experience. We discussed navigating the mental and physical aspects of the exercise and what difficulties to expect. Next came a centering activity. We instructed them to simply walk around campus and contemplate the day's work. This 45-minute preparation proved one of utmost importance. Many students assumed this particular learning block would be a waste of time, but later nearly all agreed this activity induced valuable insight for themselves and their questions. Part of this was fueled by clearing their mind of extraneous thoughts. No one doubted the energy on the sacred grounds of the Children's Home fostered sharper levels of focus.

Finally, the lodge experience began. The premise was simple. The staff set up a Chamber of Reflection. In North Carolina, the Chamber of Reflection is a place to contemplate your relationship with yourself and with the Grand Architect of the Universe. To enhance this experience, we kept the Chamber mostly bare of symbols compared to other jurisdictions that utilize it since filling it with too much symbolism seemed a distraction and unnecessary. A candle and a mirror, with a few symbols from the Masonic lectures, provided an apt setting.

After suitable time in the Chamber, the students were conducted to the lodge room, donned a white apron, gave three distinct knocks at the door, and entered to a remarkable site. The lodge, awash in candlelight, held a light haze of incense wafting through the room. The altar was prepared in the usual fashion. The students, previously instructed to proceed to the altar, gave the proper due guard, knelt and prayed for guidance, and commenced their journey. No other physical living soul shared the room. The officers' chairs were occupied by the apron and jewel of the respective station or place, and while the lodge was not open on the physical plane, it was open to the psychical and spiritual planes. The experience was mystical for many and profound for all. If we weren't such pragmatists, we'd say Magic returned to Masonry that day.

The students reported extraordinarily profound experiences, previously unimaginable to them. They stood at the altar as true Initiates. As instructed, they made their way around the room bringing their prearranged question or issue to the officers within their *inner selves*. One by one they inquired of their inner officers the wisdom, strength and beauty to help discover and understand their answers. Each *officer of their mind* responded with the insight he had to offer. Following a suitable amount of time, a bell rang indicating the evolution was complete. The initiate made his way in due form back to the mundane world where he met a staff member who debriefed him on the experience, serving as a sounding board for any lingering thoughts he wished to share.

"The most profound experience in Masonry." and "This was life-changing." were common themes and comments reiterated by most students. It was indeed a real and moving experience and it worked on multiple levels.

Grand lodges are formed from many *individual* subordinate lodges, each having its own personality, culture, and egregore. These Blue lodges make up the *super collective* of the Grand Lodge's personality, culture, and egregore. This concept can be broken down to each Blue Lodge where the *individual* Masons make up the *collective* personality, culture and egregore of the Lodge. We can break this model down yet again. Each *individual* Mason can be broken down into his own constituent parts. We each have many aspects that make up the *collective* "me." Personality typology, memories, intellect, values, life experiences, and many other traits go into the collective "you." Breaking something down into its most basic and individual parts is necessary to understand it.

A large part of contemplative work is "breaking down" the elements of yourself. The classwork leading to the primary Inner Chamber exercise focused on exactly this idea. For the exercise to achieve its full potential, each student's question had to be specific enough that an answer could be obtained, while inspiring other potential discoveries or realizations, as well.

Having the initiates carefully consider an element of themselves they didn't fully appreciate or understand, was the beginning. Explaining how they would view the issues arising from the question through the eyes of the different "officers" provided the mental tools required. The contemplative walk around campus created a mental space to work within. The Chamber of Reflection enabled them to thoughtfully focus on the question and the elements of Self it exposed. Finally, in this state they were "duly and truly prepared" for the impending lodge experience. They stood on the threshold of a life changing experience.

Think back through your life to the most revelatory experiences, events that either changed you forever, or confirmed your deepest understanding of yourself. Some may be happy occasions. Perhaps you accomplished a great physical or mental feat you believed out of your reach. Maybe a romance or birth of a child. Others were doubtless tragic events… bitter defeat, personal failure, death, or loss. These life events are turning points in our lives. They change us at our core. They shape who we become and follow us through our remaining days. In some magical way, these types of events are the catalyst making change possible. Rarely does someone experience such a transformation while performing mindless tasks.

The good news is that we needn't wait for tragedy or triumph to force these transformational occasions. With steady practice, we can create these opportunities in our mind, but this advanced work is not for the new initiate. Like everything else in life, it requires practice, patience, guidance, and effort to achieve. Yet, some techniques may help increase the efforts at hand. This is what we facilitate during the lodge exercise in the Inner Chamber Program.

The classwork leading to the exercise helped prepare each initiate mentally and spiritually. Encouragement and positive reinforcement from the instructor corps provided students confidence and *faith* they would experience a transformative exercise. The anticipation culminated in the act of stepping into the lodge. The wonderment of the room flooded the senses. Everything worked in unison to propel most initiates over a mental barrier typically difficult to cross. The confluence of the preparatory activities lifted initiates to higher awareness. The lodge room was empty, yet they were met by their inner "officers of the mind," which they'd been told to expect. In this higher state of awareness, they received answers ordinarily out of reach. The answers were always there, but only seen "through a glass darkly." But in this *different* state of consciousness, made possible by thorough preparation, the answers came easily. Whether one lifts higher or delves deeper within, the experience, without a doubt, was one of a different constitution than normal thought.

This particular exercise, at this particular Inner Chamber retreat, was made easier by the elements described, but this experience doesn't have to be limited to a once-per-year program for select initiates. It is open to all Masons throughout the world. Every brother holds the keys to this type work because it's presented in our ritual. When properly understood, our ritual provides the same tools of that fateful weekend in Oxford, North Carolina.

The sincere desire of the Middle Chamber staff is this particular aspect of Freemasonry, which has always been with us, will be introduced to all Masons again, wherever so dispersed. Then, that which is old will be new again.

Magic lies dormant in the dusty soil of our ritual. With water from the Living Springs of Truth and Light from above, it will flow again into a newness of life.

So mote it be, so mote it be, so mote it be.

Chapter Nine

The Keystone

keystone

1: the wedge-shaped piece at the crown of an arch that locks the other pieces in place

2: something on which associated things depend for support

——Merriam-Webster Dictionary

The Middle Chamber Program is the Grand Lodge of North Carolina's proactive approach to embracing a movement germinating in all American Grand Jurisdictions. The spiritual and philosophical movement within the Craft is on the rise and has been for years, driven by small pockets of a few interested brethren in localized areas. By embracing this movement, the Grand Lodge has provided guidance, oversight, and leadership to a part of the Craft that will grow with or without them.

For all the reasons mentioned throughout this book, the stage is set for a small but significant percentage of Brethren to publicly embrace the more sacred aspects of our ritualistic teachings. Currently, this mainly happens through the internet. Social media in particular, is filled with sites and groups dedicated to this growing aspect of Freemasonry. Members of these groups hail from nearly every Grand Jurisdiction. The internet has given a platform for like-minded brethren to gather virtually to discuss the Crafts' esoteric characteristics. It allows brethren from sundry locations voices on a national stage.

Before the rise of social media, brethren who sought the more recondite nature of the Craft often drifted away. Brethren seeking spiritual and philosophical enlightenment tend not to be satisfied with anything less. When they don't find it in their lodges, they give up on the fraternity to seek it elsewhere. Some may remain dues card carrying members, but more often, they simply leave the Craft. They don't typically continue to attend meetings or remain active in the fraternity in a meaningful way. Or as C.G. Jung allegorically relates it, "The dead came back from Jerusalem, where they did not find what they were looking for…"

Unfortunately, many brethren looking for deeper teachings turn to dubious sources for explanations eluding them in their lodge. This clouds their view of the fraternity's true nature and leads some down a path lacking real substance, like a stuffed bag of cotton candy, colorful and sweet to the taste, but doesn't fill the hunger.

The internet provides many opportunities to converse with seemingly wise brethren. Most new initiates have grown up in the computer age and it's rare we receive a brother who's not internet savvy. This means a great many new brethren seek answers to Masonic questions on the internet first and if unsatisfied with the results, only then resort to a phone call or an in-person discussion. This applies to nearly all questions about the fraternity, from meeting dates or Masonic jurisprudence on one end of the spectrum, to the true meaning of the Lost Word at the other.

A survey of the more esoteric sites reveals extremely diverse information being shared. Some participants share well informed, properly researched information, have beneficent intentions, and offer sage council. While others promote wild speculation, conjecture, conspiracy, and uninformed advice. Grand Lodges possess limited ability to control their members' social media interactions so the internet can be a wild west of misinformation.

Grand Lodges should consider this relatively new and growing development. What consequences may result by not providing training and guidance in *any* area of Masonry? What value is shared when new brethren are told, "Don't ask questions"? This is especially important for the esoteric aspects of the Craft. Will members who seek the meanings behind the symbolic and veiled essence of the ritual be left to find answers in the internet's dangerous waters? Who will help them discern between *fact* and *fiction?* Between Truth and speculation?

As a course on Masonic esotericism, the Middle Chamber Program cannot flourish without the Grand Lodge's support. Conversely, the Grand Lodge of North Carolina recognizes, without educational courses like the Middle Chamber Program, the fraternity may soon become a hollow shell of itself. Like opposite sides of an arch, the two are mutually supportive, with Masonic Philosophy as the keystone. By endorsing this program and giving the instructors leeway to create an aggressive and robust syllabus, the Grand Lodge provided a safe path for members to explore the mystic tie. Yet everyone has no doubt the classes continue at the will and pleasure of the Grand Master and his designated officials. If the program stepped out of bounds, the Grand Lodge would rightly take corrective action.

North Carolina brethren who search for deeper answers to Masonic questions continue to use the internet for exploration and connection with other like-minded individuals. This will never change. But they also have the Grand Lodge's officially sanctioned and managed program as the primary source of esoteric education. The brethren no longer have to rely on intuition or luck when deciding the validity of information found on the internet. More importantly, the Middle Chamber staff remain accessible to the graduates when they encounter new interpretations of the ritual. While the staff doesn't pretend to have all the answers, it does provide a rational, intelligent sounding board for questions. Based on their ongoing involvement with the staff, some alumni may even be invited to train to become teachers for the program.

The ritual ushers us into places sometimes uncomfortable and controversial. It challenges us to *know* ourselves, to confront our beliefs, to explore our exposure to ritual and symbol. Serious contemplation is required and best accomplished in the silence of one's mind. Or as written in the Psalms, "Be Still, and know that I am God."

Next, we must *dare* to change at a fundamental level. Grand Master Hiram Abiff teaches continued bravery in the face of adversity. Those with the *will* to do the hard work required, find that work can be its own reward until the final lesson is raised. Then, in the *silence* of their own temples, they may contemplate the enlightenment the ritual presents.

There are many reasons this program is successful. Chief among them is we didn't play it safe. The Grand Lodge could have issued directives limiting the scope, dictating what could be discussed and what could not. To do the lessons justice, boundaries had to be pushed. The prohibition on sectarian debate in lodges must be upheld, but when covering esoteric topics, some religious viewpoints must be permitted since much of the ritual takes place in biblical settings and the Volume of Sacred Law features prominently within our degree system. Often the intended meaning in a part of the ritual is not clear. One lesson may convey multiple alternative (even conflicting) ideas. This requires offering different interpretations to the students for later contemplation. The authors of the class textbooks, as well as our own instructors, often differ on their interpretations. This results in many Socratic discussions and presents initiates with multiple paths to explore and apply in their lives. As one of our instructors says, "It's just a story until it becomes *your* story." Single minded explanations for complex ideas become dogma. Philosophy and spirituality require the student to assimilate the lessons, not simply become a storehouse of facts and data. None of this is possible if developed under a "play it safe" cloud. The only mandate Bro. Bradshaw gave was, "Stay on Masonry."

In reality and out of necessity, the program veers into psychology, theology, history, mythology, and science. But all are grounded in the textbooks and can be tied back to Masonry. The "Stay on Masonry" mantra steers us clear from the murky waters of speculation and the teachings of other initiatic orders. Some students who attend the Middle Chamber have been involved in other initiatic orders. While this is completely acceptable, discussing the teachings or ritual of other orders are strictly off limits in class. Initiates may benefit from different systems, but our class only uses Masonic symbols, allegories. and lessons. **Stay on Masonry**.

The confluence of dwindling membership and rise in interest of the arcane knowledge in the ritual provides Grand Lodges with a challenge *and* an opportunity. Little doubt exists the fraternity is experiencing profound change. The emerging Masonic experience will be different than before and will be shaped by many competing factors. Grand Lodges proactive to these changes will guide the course of their destinies more than reactive ones who will struggle to control the evolving fraternity.

We see this class as getting back to basics. This is not an alien concept in society. Businesses, sports teams, musicians, and other entities frequently reach a crossroads, unable to continue business as usual but desperate for a new direction. A rebirth of sorts. Perhaps they have veered away from their true essence, forgetting what they do best. Perhaps they have branched out too far, attempting to become more than they intended. Often the answer to this dilemma is to get back to basics. Discover your strengths and concentrate on those core areas. Freemasonry goes in many directions and most are worthy endeavors, but our ritual and its lessons have always been with us. During this tumultuous era, returning to basic elements may be the best path forward.

There is nothing to fear in our ritual. It may not be for everyone. All are not ready to receive the lessons the Craft offers or are not willing to change. But for those who knock at the door of the lodge, are prepared in their heart, and are deemed worthy, the knowledge must be imparted. If we fear exploring our own ritual at its fundamental level, we must reevaluate ourselves as an organization.

Some in the world of social media lament the Craft is devoid of the esoteric. These include Masonic publications, books, podcasters, and rank and file members. In some jurisdictions the word "esoteric" itself is condemned or feared. Many Grand Jurisdictions spurned the term to appease the anti-Masonic fervor largely driven by fundamentalist Christians and the Southern Baptist Convention in the late-1980s and early 1990s. In some cases, the ritual was changed and its spiritual lessons were diluted to appease the critics who conflated esotericism and occultism. Despite our proximity to the Southern Baptist Convention and a number of our members active in it, the Grand Lodge of North Carolina made no ritual changes, but did move away from discussing the more spiritual aspects of our ritual to focus educational programs on the history, administration, and leadership of the fraternity. These are worthy topics but the fraternity has more to offer. Perhaps it's time to fill the void by putting that energy to work. The Most Worshipful Grand Lodge of North Carolina has done this with its Middle Chamber Program.

In this particular aspect of Masonry, the Grand Lodge of North Carolina took an active, leading role. They embraced change by providing an opportunity to explore old ideas in new ways. They allowed a return to the study of ritual at its deepest levels. They undoubtedly set the example in how a Grand Lodge can effectively create and manage a *new* program that explores *old* ideas.

Chapter Ten

The New Temple

To us the whole world is God's Temple, as is every upright heart. To establish all over the world the New Law and Reign of Love, Peace, Charity, and Toleration, is to build that [new] Temple, most acceptable to God, in erecting which Masonry is now engaged.

—Pike, Morals and Dogma

In 1626 Sir Francis Bacon's unfinished utopian novel *New Atlantis* was posthumously published. It depicts the mythical Bensalem, a utopian society. This mythical land revered an order dedicated to the pursuit of wisdom and knowledge. As described in the book, "It was the erection and institution of an order, or society, which we call Solomon's House; the noblest foundation, as we think, that ever was upon the earth, and the lantern of this kingdom. It is dedicated to the study of the works and creatures of God."[11] It was an idyllic house of learning in an idyllic society.

While unproven historically, wide speculation holds this novel influenced men who oversaw the rise of both the Royal Society and the Speculative revolution of Freemasonry over the next century. Tumultuous times during this period saw civil war, regicide, the heavy hand of Puritanism, the Restoration, the Glorious Revolution, and the

---

[11] Bacon, Francis, *Essays and New Atlantis* (Walter J. Black, Inc. 1969), 270-271.

rise of the Hanoverian Monarchy, among other events. It was an extremely chaotic period in British history. Yet this chaos created space for change. The Restoration fueled ideals of the Enlightenment and set the stage for Speculative Masonry.

Sir Francis Bacon knew his imagined world would never exist. Bensalem was fiction, a fantasy. He created an archetype of what *could* be. He envisioned the best society that could *theoretically* exist. The ensuing 100 years fell remarkably short of his vision of utopia, but it's a shame that he couldn't see how far this world *did* progress.

Like Bacon's mythical Bensalem, Freemasonry gifts us an allegorical model of the perfect lodge, representing the individual mason. By nature, it represents a *perfect* mason. Except when playing out the great lesson of the third degree, all lodge officers are present. The Kings occupy their respective stations and Grand Master Hiram Abiff is present and accounted for. The Word is secure. The craftsmen labor. The ruffians have not hatched their plot. The work is being completed. Allegorically, the ideal lodge (or Mason) is its own utopian entity. This is the normal configuration of the lodge for its meetings, representing an ideal lodge and an ideal individual Mason. But the third degree briefly leaves behind this ideal setting to step into reality, recognizing all humans are flawed. Vice, ignorance, anger, hatred, jealousy, fear… all part of human nature and the human experience. As the drama commences in the Sublime degree, the lodge exemplifies its normal, perfect state. Yet, events unfold to throw the Temple, allegorically you, into disorder. Our goal, as interpreted through the degree, is to return to perfect order. In the degree, the process of achieving balance takes less than an hour. In reality, it's probably unattainable in the life span of a man. Perfection is more goal than reality, but the third degree provides each Freemason with hope we can re-attain some level of perfection and balance we once enjoyed, when man and God lived in perfect unity. If attaining perfection is not possible, some would say we should simply give up, to not try, to do as we will. Give in to our animal passions and appetites? Many men do. But not Freemasons. We hold ourselves to higher standards. Our goal is to provide men who want to improve themselves with the working tools to do so.

The ashlars we accept into the fraternity are not perfect. When we receive them from the quarry, they are rough, but the Master Mason can see what they will become, once squared, polished, and adorned. Some stones arrive in a state of imperfection that cannot be salvaged. They are relegated to the rubbish pile and not allowed through the West Gate. But those we do choose, have the potential to be more level, more upright, and more smooth.

They make this change by working on themselves. From rough stones, they hope to attain perfection someday. Though achieving this goal is nearly impossible, they free themselves to be honed and adjusted by their mentors in the Craft. Lessons are imparted. Morals are taught. Living examples encourage us. The ritual is explained. If we are teaching these things as Masons, then understanding *will* come, and we'll see results in our members. But if we fail to teach these elements, will we be surprised if those ashlars remain in a rude and rough state?

The Middle Chamber Program doesn't solve every difficulty presented to Grand Lodges. It *does* provide a solution to one of the problems and explains to our candidates what the ritual *tries* to teach them. We don't need to invent programs to teach Masons how to interact with fellow humans or grow as individuals. Those lessons are conveyed by the ritual, albeit veiled in allegory and illustrated by symbols. The Middle Chamber Program provides a key to unlock the allegorical and symbolic materials shrouded in our ritual, one that opens up a new world of ideas and instructions to use in building their new selves.

Imagine a world where every new Mason received extensive training during their apprenticeship to build themselves in a new fashion. By using the lessons given in the degrees, most would become changed men. They would become living embodiments of the virtues, inexorably committed to *be* better men. They would provide charitable Relief because they love their fellow man. They would practice Brotherly Love and fraternalism because they desire to gather with men who inspire them. They would relentlessly pursue the Truth, realizing every man must find it himself.

They would become the best ritualists possible, making the degrees transformative experiences leaving initiates ravenous for more. They would become leaders of lodges and eventually Grand Lodges. They'd constantly rededicate themselves, striving to improve the Masonic experience for all members with every intention and all attention aimed at encouraging them to become the best men possible. *Then* we would have a foundation to build upon. *Then* we could establish the utopian Grand Lodge for the Glory of God.

Is it possible to transform today's Freemasonry into perfection? No, not completely. But it doesn't mean we shouldn't try. If perfection is unrealistic, we are honor bound to do what we can. A great place to start is with the ritual. The ritual knows nothing of membership numbers or financial reports. It never notices how brethren dress or how well it's performed. Those are institutional concerns. Ritual is simply the vessel storing the spirit of Masonry. It contains the *vital substance* or the *vivifying root* that possesses the power to change men. Although given to us all, it has been locked in an allegorical box and the keys have been misplaced. Concealed, the box lays as a forgotten relic among the rubbish of every temple. It waits to be rediscovered.

The essence of Freemasonry cannot remain hidden forever. Recent generations beg for the rubbish to be cleared so the spirit of Masonry may be renewed. The ritual, which conceals and reveals, has masterfully hidden its lessons within its allegories and symbols. But as always, to those who seek the keys, the ritual *will* unlock its secrets. And those who rediscover them, have a duty to share with those worthy to receive them.

The members and leaders wishing to see this vision of the Craft realized, must take up the mantle in their lodges and Grand Lodges. This is a call to action. Do not be one of the many who complain and bemoan the lack of esoteric education or quality ritual. Be the solution. This book exists to share how a few brethren in North Carolina banded together to build a program that meets this vision for the Craft, proving it can be realized, that it can be done. And to share with those who are willing to develop their own program, to give them a starting point on what to do and how to do it. We know the effort may be fraught with setbacks and success may seem unlikely, but we've seen positive results in North Carolina and believe we've developed a suitable model for bigger and better programs throughout the United States.

To those who want to be a part of this new movement, Rise Up! The time is upon us. The time has arrived to rediscover what has been lost. For the good of Freemasonry and your fellow men, begin to work within your jurisdictions to cultivate a new emphasis on the esoteric and philosophical aspects of our ritualistic work. Build and share your programs with others. Show your successes to instill hope in others. Let them see your failures as well so they learn what to avoid.

Together we *will* change the face of Freemasonry. Now is the time.

To all our brethren who are willing to help us with this important work, remember to **Keep the Light** and tell your story.

Afterword

Call to Action

Upon being elected Grand Master of Masons in North Carolina, I introduced myself as a "proud Masonic esotericist," fully intending to spend my year proselytizing the importance of the esoteric nature of our Craft. For the first four months of my tenure, that's exactly what I did.

As I traveled across the state, speaking with the brethren, I showcased Masonic philosophy and its importance as a regular part of our lodge meetings. I discussed how multitudes of men joined our great fraternity searching for an answer to the deep and abiding question, "Who comes here?" Instead, they found lodges focused on more mundane topics, like what meal to serve at the next meeting or when to hold the next fundraiser, or how much money was needed to pay for new carpet in the lodge. As a result, many of our brethren lost hope in ever finding an answer and left the fraternity to continue searching elsewhere.

As I met with the brethren to discuss philosophical and Masonic Truth, I discovered members throughout the state, from newly raised to fifty-year members, who'd been patiently waiting for my message… that the value of Freemasonry is not in how many members we have, but how much each man is transformed by the ritual. The value of the fraternity comes from our simple adherence to the Principal Tenets of a Mason's profession, which are Brotherly Love, Relief, and Truth.

The beginning of the year went according to plan, but Divine Providence had an additional set of tasks for me as Grand Master, a new set of designs on the trestle board. As the COVID-19 pandemic surged across our state in March, 2020, I made the difficult decision to shut down all Masonic meetings, not fully reopening the lodges again until Labor Day, 2020 (a fitting and symbolic day to resume our Masonic labors). But as the shutdown progressed in the first couple months, the path Divine Providence had laid before us became evident. Many have found only negative effects of the COVID-19 virus on our fraternity, but as an eternal optimist, I see the golden rays of light shining behind the pandemic's cloud.

On February 21-22, 2020, prior to the pandemic's rise, the Grand Lodge of North Carolina hosted the first American Masonic Renaissance Ingathering (AMRI). The brainchild of Bro. Ben Wallace and Bro. Chuck Dunning, the AMRI's purpose was to gather Masons from across the country with similar interests of bringing esoteric topics back to the forefront of lodges. Over those two days, this team of go-getters outlined methods for bringing esotericism to the Masonic masses throughout the United States. With a strategy in place, the team prepared for its next steps: a call to action and implementation of the ideas and vision developed during the AMRI meeting.

AMERICAN MASONIC RENAISSANCE INGATHERING (AMRI)

Mission Statement

To enhance the philosophic and esoteric aspects of the Masonic experience.

Vision

Every Mason will know philosophic and esoteric paths exist and are available.

That's the silver lining of this wretched virus. While I believe the brethren involved in the AMRI would eventually build the platforms, presentations, communications channels, and other elements we discussed as part of the mission and strategic vision of the meeting, the pandemic created an immediate need to continue engaging our Masonic brethren despite their inability to attend physical meetings. Today, with nearly 4000 members and more than 100 Masonic and esoteric presentations available (with new ones produced weekly) the Refracted Light Facebook group (sponsored and administered by the alumni of the AMRI) has helped fill the void left from lack of physical meetings, It fed the hunger for Masonic esoteric education.

On the flip side, not only are there more programs and presentations available online now, but many brethren who may have previously eschewed any type of online Masonic gathering are finding solace in their ability to meet and interact online with their brethren, even if only virtually. While we know online communities can never replace the in-person lodge experience, they have provided outlets for brethren to find the spiritual philosophy they craved when first preparing in their heart for the transformational nature of our ritual and fulfilling the promise to one day confidently answer the question, "Who comes here?"

Where we go from here is anyone's guess. Divine Providence has given us multiple paths to explore, from the Middle Chamber Program and it's in-person method of teaching, to the Refracted Light and its myriad online resources. Our hope is more jurisdictions find value in these tools and begin implementing them. The North Carolina Middle Chamber instructors have been pleased to meet and train interested Masons in Chicago and Houston so they can develop their own version of the program. That's why we wrote this book, to continue the education and communication process. To let our brethren throughout the Craft know:

1. There is a deeper, more esoteric, and philosophical aspect to our Craft and
2. To illustrate one method to implement a program that focuses on teaching this aspect of our ritual to interested members of our fraternity.

That is our call to action, our next steps, and our greatest hope. To see the Middle Chamber Program, or some similar, flourish in Grand Jurisdictions throughout the United States. To fill the space left by our diminished numbers and provide true value to brethren in search of further light in Masonry.

With warm fraternal regards, I am…

P. Shaun Bradshaw
Past Grand Master of Masons in North Carolina - 2020

Appendices

Suggested Reading List

Davis, Robert G. In Search of Light: A Course of Hieroglyphic and Moral Instruction for the Symbolic Lodge. (Building Stone Publishing. Guthrie, Oklahoma). 2021.

Davis, Robert G. The Mason's Words. The History and Evolution of the American Masonic Ritual. (Building Stone Publishing. Guthrie, Oklahoma). 2013.

De Hoyos. Albert Pike's Esoterika: The Symbolism of the Blue Degrees of Freemasonry. (Scottish Rite Research Society. Washington D.C.) 2005.

Dunning, Charles R. Contemplative Masonry: Basic Applications of Mindfulness, Meditation, and Imagery for the Craft. (Stone Guild Publishing, Plano Tx.) 2016.

Herd, Robert. The Initiatic Experience: Ancient Pathways that Lead to your Initiation Into Freemasonry. (Starr Publishing. Colorado Springs.) 2012.

Hornsby, Tony. The Rough and Rugged Road: Personal Reflections on Initiation. (LVX Endeavours. Northglenn, Co.). 2013.

Mackey, Albert G. A Lexicon of Freemasonry. (Mass and Brothers, Philadelphia). 1885.

Mackey, Albert G. An Encyclopedia of Freemasonry. (The Masonic History Company, Chicago.). 1921.

MacNulty, Kirk W. Contemplating Craft Freemasonry. Working the Way of the Craftsman. (Plumbstone, Washington D.C.). 2018.

MacNulty, Kirk W. The Way of the Craftsman: A Search for the Spiritual Essence of Craft Freemasonry. Deluxe Edition. (Plumbstone. Washington D.C.) 2017.

Steinmetz, George. Freemasonry, It's Hidden Meaning. (Macoy Publishing and Masonic Supply. Richmond Va.). 1948.

Tresner, Jim. But I Digress. A Collection of Masonic Musings and Writings From Dr. Jim Tresner. (Starr Publishing LLC, Colorado Springs Colorado). 2012.

Wilmshurst, Walter L. The Masonic Initiation. (William Rider & Son. London, England). 1924.

Wilmshurst, Walter L. The Meaning of Masonry. (Crown Publishers. London England) 1927.

Middle Chamber Team Members

Most Worshipful Shaun Bradshaw

Shaun Bradshaw is a founder and Vice-President of Zenergy Technologies and an internationally recognized speaker in the Agile and Testing industries. Shaun was raised a Master Mason in 1997 and served as Master of Stokesdale Lodge No. 428 in 2003. In 2020, Shaun served as Grand Master of the Grand Lodge of AF & AM of North Carolina. He is also an active member in several appendant and concordant Masonic organizations.

WORSHIPFUL RANDY BROWNING, III

Brother Randy is a Past Master of Blackmer Lodge No. 127 and Sophia Lodge No. 767, as well as a member of Wilkerson College Lodge No. 760. In an ever-changing world, Brother Randy believes Masonry is as relevant today as it ever has ever been. He desires to help other Masons realize the many ways Freemasonry can improve their lives.

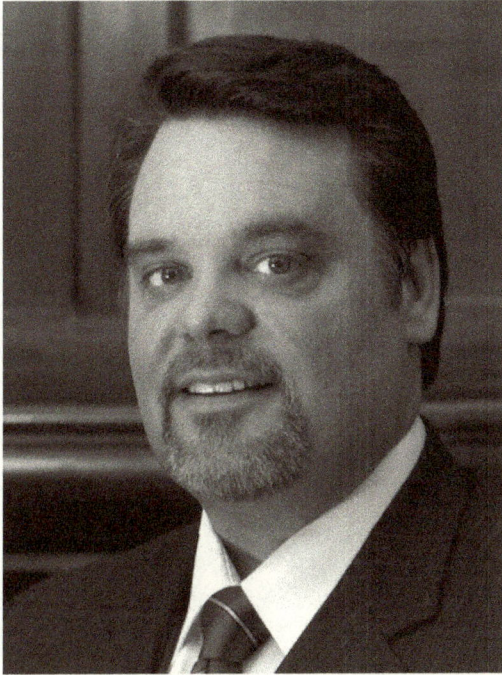

WORSHIPFUL MIKE DANIELS

Brother Michael Daniels, 33°, KYCH, served as Grand Commander of the Grand Commandery of Knights Templar in North Carolina from 2019-2021 and serves on the Grand Lodge Committee on Masonic Education. He is Director of Academics for the Davie Academy and instructs for Wilkerson College. He is a Past Master of Bush Hill Lodge No. 732 in Archdale, a charter member of Sophia Lodge, President of the Greensboro Masonic Temple Company, Past Governor of the Piedmont York Rite College, Director of the Work for Greensboro Scottish Rite, and a Knight of the Royal Order of Scotland. Brother Daniels is classically educated and holds a Bachelor of Science degree in Psychology and graduate work in Adult Learning and Instructional Design.

BROTHER MATTHEW PARKER

Brother Parker is a member of Wendell Lodge No. 565 in Wendell, the Raleigh York Rite Bodies, the Raleigh Valley of the Scottish Rite, Allied Masonic Degrees, Shriners, and several other Masonic Organizations. Bro. Parker is the founder of the North Carolina Masonic Research Society and a founding member of the Refracted Light Facebook Group. He speaks frequently to Masonic organizations both locally and internationally, focusing on the allegories and symbolism of the Craft ritual emphasizing the path toward self-development through contemplative practices. Bro. Parker serves as Student Services Coordinator for the Middle Chamber Program.

WORSHIPFUL BEN WALLACE

Brother Wallace, a Past Master of Blackmer Lodge No. 127, Wilkerson College Lodge No. 760, and Sophia Lodge No. 767, is a veteran speaker on several topics with specific interests in the allegory and symbolism of Freemasonry, Masonic educational outreach, and Masonic history.

Allegory & Symbolism Lectures Full Outline

The Allegory & Symbolism Lectures, a precursor to the full Middle Chamber Program, followed the basic premises of the ritual and symbols as described in Wilmshurst's *The Meaning of Masonry* and MacNulty's *The Way of the Craftsman*. The outline of ritual topics and symbols discussed in these early lectures is presented here to illustrate information presented to the attendees. From this outline, the Middle Chamber Program instructors expanded the concepts and developed standardized **Instructor Notes** for each degree and section currently taught.

INTRODUCTION

- The lesson of the Northeast Corner
    - Veiled in Allegory, Illustrated by Symbols
    - When do we explain the allegory and symbolism to the new Entered Apprentice?
    - Provide an in-depth explanation of allegory, symbolism and correspondences
- The Western Mystery Tradition: Its development & comparisons to Freemasonry
- Masonic History
- Masonic Philosophy
    - Explain that many Masonic philosophies exist and provide examples of the more popular ones
    - Briefly explain the philosophy of Wilmshurst, MacNulty, Steinmetz, etc....
    - Explain this program is based on these Masonic philosophers. Others may not be wrong, but this program is based on the lodge as a model of Man and his constituent aspects.

ENTERED APPRENTICE DEGREE

- Explain the main takeaways of the Entered Apprentice degree
  - The Ego and Materialism
  - The Virtues (Cardinal/Heavenly)
  - The Principal Tenets
- Explain the main aspects of the degree
  - The Divestiture
  - The Reception
  - Who Comes Here?
  - The purpose of the Guide
  - The Prayer at the Center of the Lodge
- Explain key symbols of the degree
  - The Lights
  - The Square and Compasses (provide Pike's explanation)
  - The Apron
  - The Demand
  - The Northeast Corner (review)
  - The Working Tools
- Discuss main points of the Lecture
  - The Principal Tenets
  - The Virtues
  - The Point within the Circle

FELLOW CRAFT DEGREE

- Review key aspects of the Degree
- Discuss main points of the Lecture
  - The Columns: Dualities and Trinities/Kabbalistic explanations
  - The Three Steps: Physical, Psychical, Spiritual
  - The Five Steps: Sacred Architecture and the Illusion of the 5 Senses
  - The Seven Steps

- The Exoteric explanation vs. the Kabbalistic explanation
- Trivium/Quadrivium: The importance of education in relation to living a balanced life
  - An esoteric explanation of the symbols of the Ephramites story
    - Veils/Rivers/Guards
    - Corn/Wine/Oil
    - Intro to Sacrifice (Jeptha)
  - The Middle Chamber

MASTER MASON DEGREE

- Brief review of the First Section
- Detailed review of key symbols and allegories of the Second Section
  - Introduce the Officers and their Correspondences (MacNulty)
  - Why is the Junior Warden's chair empty?
  - The Entrance
  - The Prayer
  - The Ruffians
  - The Assault
  - The Rubbish of the Temple
  - The Brow of the Hill
  - The Search
  - The number 12 and role of the Fellow Crafts
  - The Raising
- Discuss main points of the Lecture
  - The Lion's Paw (including an astrological explanation)
  - The Temple

You Can't Rush Enlightenment

The following Grand Oration was delivered by Bro. Ben Wallace at the 2020 Annual Communication of the Most Worshipful Grand Lodge of North Carolina. It is presented here as a call to action for what Freemasonry can be, if and when, Grand Lodge leaders take the esoteric aspects of our rituals seriously.

GRAND ORATION

Grand Master, Grand Line Officers, Distinguished Guests and Brethren all. Thank you for the opportunity to share with you some thoughts on the process by which we, as Masons, attempt to change the lives of the men who knock upon the door of Freemasonry.

If you were lucky enough to hear our Grand Master speak at one of the district meetings, you will recall he referred to the degrees of Freemasonry as a "Transformative Experience." Transformative in that we theoretically receive a man into the Craft and "by the Secrets of our Art" transform him into a better version of himself. This does not mean that he simply learns to act in a better manner... but he actually becomes better. There is a subtle but imperative difference. The former is a method that allows us to merely act better when certain circumstances dictate. The latter is a fundamental change to a man's essence.

Freemasonry has, within the corpus of its ritual, elements we as leaders of the Craft use to teach our initiates how to facilitate this process. This is the "Secrets of our Art" which we refer to in the Entered Apprentice degree. However, our ritual also tells us these secrets are "veiled in allegory and illustrated by symbols." As leaders of your lodges, it's your duty to unlock the *veiled and illustrated* aspects of the ancient Craft for our initiates by applying the "Secrets of our Art" and thus allow them to receive the transformative experience our Grand Master refers to. However, we often fail at this task.

The reasons for this are many and time does not permit me to enumerate them all, so we will skip most of the history in order to concentrate on the problem and the solutions.

In our present system, we rush our candidates through the degrees at an extremely rapid pace. Freemasonry has been called a progressive art. This alludes to the idea that an initiate should not progress to the next degree until he has learned the lessons of his current degree. A Fellow Craft uses the lessons he learned as an Entered Apprentice in order to understand the lessons of the Fellow Craft degree. In turn those lessons are used to understand the great Truths we are to acquire from the sublime degree Master Mason. If one fails to learn the progressive lessons as he goes, the lessons of the subsequent degree cannot be effectively incorporated, and the whole concept falls like a temple built on sand instead of the solid cornerstone that we all stood upon when we were placed in the Northeast corner of the Lodge. By what reasoning would someone attempt to learn Trigonometry without first having mastered addition, subtraction, multiplication and division? Such an attempt would be a recipe for failure. Yet this is analogous to the manner in which we train our initiates.

Let us not be confused here brethren, these "Secrets of our Art" we are discussing go well beyond memorizing the words and actions of the ritual. These secrets are the means by which we unlock the aspects which our ritual refers to as being veiled and illustrated. The word veiled clearly indicates they are hidden. That is, they are not plainly stated in the ritual, they are beyond it. The ritual as we perform it is not veiled (from us), yet it contains the veiled aspect. This we clearly say to the candidate when he is standing in the Northeast corner. So, if these secrets are outside of and in addition to the material contained in the Official Standard of Work and the Bahnson manual, how are we to know them ourselves so that we can in turn teach them to our novices? The answer is you have to be taught this from your lodge leaders and for nearly all of us, this has simply not been the case. These veiled aspects of the Craft are simply no longer being passed on, only the unveiled parts of the ritual are, that being what is contained in the pages of the OSW and the Bahnson Manual.

There are two important distinctions I feel compelled to make.

First that everything you need to know in order to fulfill your quest for enlightenment is contained within the ritual, although it isn't explained in clear text of the Bahnson Manual or the cyphered work of the OSW. It is veiled in allegory and illustrated by symbols. It is our job to unveil the allegory and decipher the symbols. Esotericists often fall into the trap of looking outside of Masonry for secrets, which are contained within their own ritual. The Great Light in Masonry would remind them that "Neither shall they say Lo here or, lo there, for behold, the kingdom of God is within you." This lesson can be applied here in the fact the secret of the Lost Word is with us always and the key to finding it is hidden within our ritual.

The second distinction is that you simply cannot begin to unravel the hidden lessons of the ritual until you know the ritual. If you want to become a fully developed (that is, *transformed*) Master Mason, you must first learn all of the ritual, and then use the "Secrets of our Art" to decipher and comprehend its hidden meaning.

So far, we have discussed the fact that:

- Freemasonry is meant to be a transformative experience.
- The means by which we teach this transformation is concealed within the ritual.
- It is the job of the leaders of the Lodge to teach this.
- They should do so by using the "Secrets of our Art".
- Often the current lodge leaders were not taught these secrets themselves.
- This causes a breakdown in the system.
- Everything we need to know for this work is contained within the ritual and it is possible to decipher it.
- And finally, the first step in doing this must be to learn all of the ritual.

Now let's spend a few minutes discussing the process by which we currently advance candidates. In our current system there seems to be an all-out sprint from petitioning to raising. I don't have data on this, but my experience is that a *good* candidate will be ready to advance from Entered Apprentice to Fellow Craft in 6-8 weeks and then from Fellow Craft to Master Mason in 4-6 weeks. Some are quicker and some are slower, but the point is we are moving them through these degrees at a very rapid pace. Why? If Masonry truly is a progressive art, and if we can agree that one needs to actually learn the lessons, not just the words of a catechism in order to advance, then by what reasoning can we expect this to happen in a matter of weeks? The answer is that we can't. The Entered Apprentice is expected to both learn and apply in his life matters related to materialism, the false self or ego, the tenets, the heavenly and the cardinal virtues, and his place in the universe. All of this is in addition to memorizing the words of his catechism. The short duration between the degree of Fellow Craft and Master Mason holds the same challenge. Lessons of balance and equilibrium, the Noe-Platonic aspects of man, sacred geometry, man's understanding of his place in the world related to his limited senses, the trivium and quadrivium of the classical world, an introduction to sacrifice and finally how to journey into the innermost recesses of his being, are all presented to the candidate and at least a basic understanding of them is critical to the final lesson of transcendence presented to him in the Master Mason degree. To think these lessons can be grasped, let alone implemented in a Fellow Craft in mere weeks is foolishness. Yet we do it anyway. Again, I ask, "Why?"

We even have a regulation (73-6) in the code which states…

REG. 73-6 DEFAULT. If an Entered Apprentice or a Fellow Craft fails to present himself prepared for advancement within six months after initiation or passing, he must apply in writing to the lodge for advancement. In the event more than Two (2) years have passed since his Initiation or Passing, the application shall be forwarded to the Grand Secretary and referred to a Committee of Investigation whose report shall be filed before a ballot can be had thereon. The Grand Secretary shall order a criminal background check of the applicant, and information with respect to the petitioner as he may possess. (This regulation amended, effective January 1, 2018.)

If we can agree that in Masonry there are secrets which are "veiled in allegory and illustrated by symbols" and we are to use the "Secrets of our Art" to teach them to our initiates and that it is critical to do this before the candidates are advanced to the next degree, then it is foolhardy to think that we are accomplishing this within the compressed timeline in which we routinely advance our initiates. Does anyone really think that we are succeeding in this intention? Perhaps this is why our attrition rate is so great? Perhaps if we were to teach these lessons in addition to the words we use to conceal them, we may deliver greater value and entice a few more of our young brethren to stay the course. How can we possibly think skipping these lessons and rushing to an end will pay benefits? Of course, this theory presupposes the benefit, doesn't it? If the benefit we seek is directed toward the candidate and his self-improvement during his journey toward transformation, then it makes no sense whatsoever. However, perhaps I have confused the objective. If the goal is to get him his dues card, then things become more clear. A dues-card **[hold mine up for effect]**.

The word "card" implies membership in an administrative sense. It is a symbol which allows a brother to attend lodge, to visit other lodges and enjoy the benefits of membership. Since this august body has thrice refused to allow Entered Apprentices to attend lodge meetings by giving Worshipful Masters the option of opening on the 1st degree, then perhaps rushing them through the degrees in order to allow them to attend and to receive Masonic instruction within the sacred retreat of the Master Mason's lodge has some validity. But we have already established we are not teaching these *veiled and illustrated* lessons because they have become mostly lost to us.

Likely the first word named on this card, "Dues," gives us a better clue as to the reason for our rush to the raising. For once a member crosses the coveted finish line of the 3rd degree, once we have shared the great mystical and spiritual lesson of the ages with our candidate, we can then... get... his... damned... money! (And often, cram him into an Officers' chair.)

Our leadership is progressive and proactive, and they are constantly, rightly urging us to make Masons, not just members. They understand the value of initiating men of high quality into this ancient and honorable fraternity. Money is not their main concern... good Masons are their concern. We have somehow developed this culture of expeditious candidate advancement, however it happened long before any of them knocked at the door of Freemasonry. So, it is not their fault. Neither is it your fault, for the same reason. But I have hope that someday this system can be amended to better fit the development of the candidates, not the needs of the budget.

So far, we have been discussing the problem. I would now like to move on to possible solutions.

In a perfect world, perhaps our rules and culture would allow initiates to advance at their own pace. Perhaps they would be allowed to attend lodge while remaining in the degree in which they are currently studying until their mentors had decided they were ready to advance, regardless of timelines, expectations, and Regulation 73.6. Then, when they were properly prepared, they could apply to move to the lessons of the next degree. Then, during the degree, when the principal officers ask the candidate's guide if he is "worthy and well qualified" and "duly and truly prepared," we could truthfully answer "yes," knowing the question applies to the state of his inner development, not just the way he is wearing his clothing and the fact he had memorized the words of a catechism. But a time such as this is going to require a cultural shift, which is still far in the future.

In the meantime, we have this system in which we currently reside. For the foreseeable future we will still rush candidates through and accept the devaluation of the Essence of Freemasonry that comes along with it.

But there is Hope!

There is a way that we can make the current system work better. Not perfectly, but better. Just as the Substitute Word is a pale surrogate for the Lost Word, we will have to make do with a proxy system until we evolve back to a true initiatic system as I believe was envisioned by our forefathers.

If we cannot slow our current system down enough to teach our initiates the lessons as they advance at their natural rate, our only recourse is to teach them after they have been raised to the sublime degree of Master Mason. If we are forced by our own rules and culture to gallop them through the degrees, then once we have done this, we simply must stop, catch our breath, and then revisit the Universal Truths they were supposed to have learned as they progressed through the degrees. Move them through at the corporate pace if we must, but then go back through the work and teach them what they were denied, due to our current zealousness for members. As leaders in your lodges, it is incumbent upon you to teach them!

Let us again review.

You were earlier introduced to the concept that:

- Freemasonry is meant to be a transformative experience
- The means by which we teach this transformation is concealed within the ritual and it's the job of the leaders of the Lodge to teach this using the "Secrets of our Art" to the younger members
- Often the current lodge leaders were not taught these secrets themselves
- Everything we need to know for this work is contained within the ritual
- It is possible to decipher it and the first step in doing this must be to learn all of the ritual.

To this we add:

- We advance our candidates at a pace that doesn't allow them time to learn the lessons fully.
- This culture and its rules are not likely to change anytime soon.
- If we are going to really teach our initiates, we have to find a substitute way of instructing them.
- That way is to revisit the teachings of the degrees after they have been raised to the sublime degree.
- This responsibility falls on the leaders of the lodges.

At this point you are likely thinking there is a problem, and you would be correct. Since the system has been broken in a manner that Freemasonry is no longer teaching the *veiled and illustrated* lessons and the "Secret of our Art" by which we are to teach them, you were likely never taught this yourself! And if you were never taught this, how can you be expected to teach others. Herein lies the dilemma. The answer is a very long and multifaceted discussion, but today we are going to discuss three simple things you can do to fulfil your obligation to teach the members of your lodge. I will very briefly discuss the Speakers Bureau, the Middle Chamber Program, and our ritual.

The Speakers Bureau is easily accessible through the Educational Resources portal of the Grand Lodge website. It offers a very easy way to bring a real live speaker to your lodge. Speakers offer a variety of topics, all of which are informative and interesting. The topics offered by speakers are listed on the site and it is easy to find the ones that discuss the more esoteric and transformative aspects of the ritual. Even if you are not well versed in these aspects of initiatic development, this tool offers you an easy way to bring it into your lodge, for both your own development and that of your candidates and members.

The Middle Chamber is a more in-depth course on the spiritual and philosophical aspects of the ritual. It is a yearlong study in this work and is the product of the forward-thinking nature of your Grand Lodge. To my knowledge, our Grand Lodge is the first in the country to offer this type of training. Even if you are not personally interested in pursuing this class, simply being aware of it will allow you to offer the experience to the members of your lodge and thus take the burden of teaching off of your shoulders.

The last is working within your ritual. What I am suggesting goes well beyond merely practicing the words and movements. The idea is to discuss the ritual in depth and what meaning it holds for you. I have seen this used to great effect. WB Dale Goforth, the Master of my home lodge, Blackmer Lodge No. 127, has utilized this technique and the results were impressive. As Masonic Education, he simply started reciting parts of the ritual and every few sentences he would stop and ask what the members thought those lines might be alluding to. The range and depth of answers was refreshing. In the absence of more structured education, I urge you to use this technique. It requires almost no pre-planning or logistics. Simply discuss the meaning of the ritual, in depth, in open Lodge. Even answers that are off base offer a lesson in themselves. Keep in mind everything you need to recover the Lost Word is contained within your ritual, it is just "veiled in allegory, and illustrated by symbols."

Brethren, these are three easy ways you can begin the process of changing our culture from a membership and numbers driven mentality, into a Temple of Wisdom, which teaches its initiates how to transform themselves into enlightened Master Masons. I urge you to put these things into practice. It is your obligation and your duty to do so. I have every confidence you will succeed.

Thank you for your time.

Grand Master, thank you for the opportunity to speak on this matter.

Fraternally and Sincerely,

Ben Wallace... Master Mason

NOTES:

NOTES: